AF377709

1939-1945
WORLD WAR TWO

AUTHOR

Carlo Cucut was born in Nole (TO) in 1955. He has cultivated a passion for history since he was a boy and over the years he has deepened this interest by dedicating himself to historical research. He has published articles on the magazines: "Storia del XX Secolo", "Storie & Battaglie", "Milites" and "Ritterkreuz". In the editorial field he has published several volumes for Marvia Edizioni: "Penne Nere sul confine orientale. Storia del Reggimento Alpini "Tagliamento" 1943-1945", winner of the De Cia Prize; "Attilio Viziano. Memories of a war correspondent"; "Forze Armate della RSI sul fronte orientale"; "Forze Armate della RSI sul fronte occidentale"; "Forze Armate della RSI sulla linea Gotica"; "Alpini nella Città di Fiume 1944-1945". For the Gruppo Modellistico Trentino he published "Le forze armate della RSI 1943-1945. Ground Forces".

FONTI FOTOGRAFICHE:

ESTONIA: http://nelsonlambert.blogspot.com/2012/06/estonian-armour-1919.html
https://ajapaik.ee/photo
http://eag.vanatehnika.ee/ewarmee.html
www.ra.ee/fotis/index.php
http://tankfront.ru
www.rindeleht.ee/foorum/php
tratto da "Tankai Lietuvos kariuomenėje 1924–1940 m.", op. cit. in bibliografia
http://aviarmor.net/tww2/armored
www.militaar.net
www.smartage.pl/crossley-armoured-car
https://reibert.info/threads
www.muis.ee/catalogue#Tulemused
www.vanadpildid.net/paide
www.osta.ee/soomusautod-auto-tanki-rugement
www.e-varamu.ee/searchresults

LETTONIA: https://www.securityguard.lv/2020/01/blog-post_30.html
http://tankfront.ru/neutral/latvia/photo
https://wp-lv.wikideck.com/Brunautomobilis
https://vesture.eu/Attels:Tankisti.png
www.antik-war.lv/viewtopic.php
www.zudusilatvija.lv/objects/
www."Sargs".lv/lv/latvijas-neatkaribas-kars
www.la.lv/foto-militaras-parades-latvija-cauri-laikiem
https://commons.wikimedia.org
www.alternativefinland.com/wp-content/uploads
https://wofmd.com/2018/04/27/daimler-plattformwagen

LITUANIA: https://forum.axishistory.com
http://arecibo-camo.blogspot.com/2011/03/"PRAGARAS"-"Perkunas"-ir-kt.html
tratto da "Lietuvos kariuomenė laikinojoje sostinėje 1919–1940 m.", op. cit. In bibliografia
tratto da: VYTAUTO DIDŽIOJO KARO MUZIEJUS 2018 op. cit. In bibliografia
tratto da "Tankai Lietuvos kariuomenėje 1924–1940 m.", op. cit. in bibliografia
https://picturehistory.livejournal.com/313760.html
https://picturehistory.livejournal.com/313760.html
www.facebook.com/senosfotografijos/photos/lietuvos-kariuomenès
http://tankfront.ru/neutral/litva/photo.html

Title: **ARMOURED UNITS OF THE BALTIC REPUBLICS ESTONIA-LATVIA-LITHUANIA** Code.: **WTW-033 EN**
By Carlo Cucut
ISBN code: 978-88-93278386 First edition march 2022
Text: English Nr. of images: 185 layout: 177,8x254mm Cover & Art Design: Luca S. Cristini

WITNESS TO WAR (SOLDIERSHOP) is a trademark of Luca Cristini Editore, via Orio, 35/4 - 24050 Zanica (BG) ITALY.

WITNESS TO WAR

ARMORED UNITS OF THE BALTIC REPUBLICS
ESTONIA - LATVIA - LITHUANIA

FROM INDEPENDENCE TO SOVIET OCCUPATION: 1918 – 1940

PHOTOS & IMAGES FROM WORLD WARTIME ARCHIVES

CARLO CUCUT

BOOKS TO COLLECT

INDICE

▲ The armored car *"Estonia"* with its crew during the War of Independence.

INDEPENDENCE OF THE BALTIC STATES

Three years after the beginning of the First World War, the Russian Empire in 1917 was experiencing one of the most dramatic moments in its history. The numerous defeats on the battlefields, which had led to the loss of Poland, Ukraine and part of the Baltic countries, the serious internal crisis with the exhausted population, the growing popularity of Marxist movements and the violent suppression of street riots, were the precursors of the October Revolution, which culminated in the fall of the Tsar, the end of the Russian Empire and the birth of the Russian Soviet Socialist Federative Republic (RSFSR).

The Estonian, Latvian and Lithuanian independence movements took the opportunity of the outbreak of the Russian Revolution to claim their national identity, declaring independence during 1918. Lithuania declared its independence on February 16, 1918, Estonia on February 24, 1918 and Latvia on November 18, 1918. Because of the different military situations on the territory, the proclamation of independence had different effects on the single nations.

In Estonia, occupied by German troops since October 1917, independence was not recognized by the German Empire, which however did not hinder independence movements. With the peace of Brest-Litovsk of March 3, 1918, which sanctioned the end of the war between the German Empire and the RSFSR, German troops abandoned Estonia, which was then reoccupied by the Bolshevik troops of the Red Army. Therefore began a bloody and bloody war of independence between Estonians, supported by some western states, and Russians, ended only with the signing of the peace treaty of Tartu on February 2, 1920, in which was sanctioned the definitive birth of the Estonian Republic.

A few days after proclaiming independence, Latvia was invaded by the troops of the Red Army that, not opposed by any military force, occupied most of the territory, including the capital Riga in January 1919. Only a small area located southwest of Liepaja resisted to the Bolshevik attack. Thanks to the agreement stipulated with Germany, volunteers and weapons arrived and allowed the constitution of units able to oppose the Russian advance. The "Baltische Landswehr", constituted by Baltic Germans, and the presence of the German "Eiserne Division", allowed the Latvian troops to reconquer, in the spring of 1919, Riga and the southern Latvia. With the help of Estonian troops was then reconquered the northern Latvia and, in January 1920, the new Latvian National Army drove out the Bolsheviks from the eastern territory. On February 1, 1920 was signed an armistice between Latvia and the RSFSR, followed by the Treaty of Riga on August 11, 1920, which established the full independence of the Republic of Latvia.

Lithuania, at the date of the proclamation of independence, was occupied by German troops and was part of the Ober Ost, consisting of Latvia, Lithuania and part of Belarus, following the peace treaty of Brest-Litovsk. Only in November 1918 German troops began to withdraw from Lithuania, which was immediately invaded by the Red Army. The Lithuanian armed forces, quickly trained, supported by the retreating Germans, blocked the Bolshevik advance and, with a counter-offensive, managed to drive the invader out of the borders. Only the area of Vilnius, proclaimed capital of the new Republic, was not reconquered, remaining in the hands of the Poles. On July 12, 1920 was signed the peace treaty between Lithuania and the RSFSR. In the autumn of 1920 a short war broke out between Lithuania and Poland for the control of the city of Vilnius and the surrounding area, which saw Poland excel. Following the war the provisional capital of Lithuania was established in the city of Kaunas. In January 1923 Lithuania occupied the German city of Memel (Klaipėda), an important industrial center of the smaller Lithuania, thus gaining the only access to the Baltic Sea of the young republic. It was Lithuania's last conflict.

▲ Nice image of the armored car *"Estonia"* where you can verify the use of trench badges for armor.

▼ The armored car *"Vanapagan"* with its crew during a break in the fighting.

ARMORED UNITS OF ESTONIA

To face the troops of the Red Army on 28 November 1918, the date of the beginning of the Estonian War of Independence, apart from a few units of the paramilitary militia of the Estonian Defence League "Kaitseliit", the newborn Estonian army "Eesti maavägi" could oppose very few forces. Under the energetic leadership of General Johan Laidoner, who had been in charge of the Eesti maavägi since 23 December, thousands of recruits were enlisted and trained, but the numerical and material supremacy of the Red Army remained 3 to 1. In mid-January 1919 the advance of the Bolshevik troops had arrived at about thirty kilometers from the capital Tallinn. Some western nations responded to the request for aid from the Estonian government; first of all Great Britain, which sent a naval force and numerous weapons, followed by contingents of Finnish, Swedish and Danish volunteers. It was also created a battalion of Baltic-Germans that, unlike what happened in Latvia, fought alongside the Estonians against the Red Army. Since, apart from rifles, machine guns and cannons, neither armored cars nor tanks had been delivered, under the impulse of Johan Pitka[1] at local companies the first armored cars and numerous armored trains were built, which were essential for the defense and subsequent counter-offensive of the Estonian army. In December 1918 at the Tallinna Sadamatehas, a naval workshop located within the port area of Tallinn, based on the drawings of the engineer Ludwig Saukas and with the technical coordination of Lieutenant A. Uus, the first armored car was built. Uus, was built the first national armored car called "*Estonia*[2]" and delivered by the end of the year to the army. It was built on the basis of the frame of a 3-ton truck brand Federal, using for the armor plates used in naval construction and trench shields on a wooden frame. The armament was remarkable, consisting of a 37mm Hotchkiss cannon in a rotating turret, 2 rear 7.62mm Maxin machine guns and the possibility of placing another light machine gun next to the driver's seat. The result was a vehicle of considerable weight and with an engine of low power, reason why the Estonia was used only on the roads of Tallinn in service in the Kaitseliit. After the construction of the Estonia began immediately the manufacture of a new armored car, this time on a Renault chassis, with the fighting compartment uncovered. This allowed to save about a ton of weight and to make the vehicle more mobile. It was called "*Tasuja*" and entered service in January 1919. Deployed on the southern front, it was lost during the fighting near the town of Orava on March 23, 1919. Since the project of the armored cars was considered positive, at the turn of December 1918 and January 1919, Captain Uus was assigned the task of building more vehicles for the Estonian army, a task that he undertook with the collaboration of engineer Saukas. A new project of armored cars was then developed for the construction of six identical vehicles, with the start of work in January 1919. Apart from the first armored car built on a Packard chassis, all the remaining five vehicles were assembled on the chassis of the 3-ton truck of the British company AEC[3], using steel plates with thicknesses varying from 6 to 10 mm for the armor, while heavy wooden beams were used for the floor. The armored cars were identified as M1918/19. These vehicles also received a name:

• "*Wahur*" on Packard chassis: completed in February 1919, in service from March 15th
• "*Toonela*" on AEC chassis: completed in April 1919, in service from April 22nd

1 Johan Pitka was an Estonian military among the founders of the League of Defense. During the War of Independence he was the architect of the construction of armed trains, assuming the command of one of them, and the first armored cars. He contributed to the organization of the Navy reaching the rank of Rear Admiral.

2 A few years ago, a working replica of the Estonia armored car was built and paraded on the occasion of military parades or national celebrations with the presence of Kaitseliit soldiers in their original uniforms.

3 AEC - Associated Equipment Company, a British manufacturer of trucks and buses established in 1912 and owned by Volvo since 1979.

- *"Wibaune"* on AEC chassis: completed in April 1919, in service since April 23rd
- *"Kalevipoeg"* on AEC chassis: completed in April 1919, in service since April 25th
- *"Kotkasilm"* on AEC chassis: completed in January 1920, in service since March
- *"Erilane"* on AEC chassis: completed in January 1920, in service in March (from October 20th, 1920 it was renamed *"Lembit"*)

All of the six armored cars had the same armament, a 37 mm Hotchkiss gun in a rotating turret, two 7.62 mm Maxin machine guns at the rear and the possibility to install a 7.7 mm Madsen machine gun at the front.

Due to high fuel consumption, the range of the armored cars was just over 100 kilometers, with tanks that could hold about 130 liters of fuel. The maximum speed on asphalted roads, or with hard ground, was 45 km/h and in reverse 10 km/h. Only the Estonian could reach 15 km/h in reverse.

The speed in reverse was important because in combat, in order to exploit the best rear armament, the armored cars moved backwards. In this way, in addition to the greater volume of fire available, not only was the engine compartment, which had little armor, protected, but it was possible to retreat quickly given the little, or no, mobility off the road, being all vehicles with only 2-wheel drive, which, in case of failure of the offensive action, would have prevented the vehicle from changing direction without getting stuck.

In April 1919 Estonia was rebuilt based on the design of the new armored cars.

On 3 March 1919 the Finnish volunteers of the "Pohjan Pojat" regiment captured a Peerless armoured truck armed with a 40mm anti-aircraft gun from the Bolsheviks. When the volunteers left Estonia in April 1919 the truck was handed over to the Estonian army that had it rebuilt as an armored car, equipped with a rotating turret with a 37 mm cannon and called *"Pisuhänd"*.

On the initiative of the 6th Infantry Regiment, an armored car called *"Vanapagan"* was built at the depot of the narrow-gauge railway of Pärnu (Parnu kitsaroopmelise raudtee veduridepoo), based on the project of the engineer Jaarats. Built on the chassis of a Delahaye truck captured from the Russians, using iron sheets 7 mm thick on a wooden frame, it was initially armed with two Lewis 7.7 mm machine guns, then implemented with another Maxim 7.62 mm machine gun. It was assembled by February 1919 and used exclusively by the Regiment.

On 20 February 1919 was formed the Soomusrongide Divisjon, the division that grouped all armored trains built. On April 14 the Soomusautode Kolonn was constituted, a unit that grouped all armored vehicles at the time in service in the Estonian Army. Its main function was to provide for the repair of the armored cars, to send the materials necessary for the operation of the vehicles to the front and to provide administrative management of military and vehicles in service. The first commander was Captain August Nieländer, replaced on October 10, 1919 by Lieutenant Albert Ojasson. It was then built a repair shop whose command was entrusted to Captain Uus.

The armored cars were mainly used in support of infantry units and in raiding/police operations, there were few combat actions that saw them employed, noteworthy is that of *"Kalevipoeg"*, under the command of Swedish Captain Lundborg[4], which led to the conquest of Pskov on May 25, 1919. Also of note are the actions of the *"Vanapagan"* in support of the infantrymen of the 6th Regiment between June 20 and 22 and sporadic battles sustained by the armored cars *"Toonela"* and *"Wibaune"* on the southern front in the last ten days of June. On 25 June *"Toonela"* was stationed on the Riga-Pskov highway guarding the Cesis Bridge.

On 24 July 1919, during a series of clashes with Red Army troops, the Estonia armored car damaged a Russian Austin-Putilov armored car forcing the crew to abandon the vehicle, which was

4 Albert Paul Muni Einar Lundborg was a Swedish officer who, after participating as a volunteer in the ranks of the White Army during the Finnish Civil War, in February 1919 joined the Latvian army fighting against the Red Army. He commanded the armored car *"Kalevipoeg"* in the taking of the city of Pskov. He was decorated with the Estonian Freedom Cross.

captured and redeployed, after repair, by the Estonian Army under the name *"Tasuja"*, as the second Estonia-built armored car lost in March.

On 23 August 1919 the Soomusautode Kolonn was placed within the Soomusrongide Divisjon. As the number of armored cars in service grew armored vehicle groups were formed, each with three vehicles at its disposal.

In the last months of the war two more armored cars were captured from the Red Army, immediately redeployed by the Estonian units, an Austin-Putilov, which was called *"Suur Tõll"*, and a Fiat-Izhorski called *"Wambola"*.

Between August and September 1919 the British landed in Tallinn 6 Mark V Composite[5] tanks to be delivered to the White Army of General Judenič, together with a contingent of 48 soldiers with the task of training the White Russians in their use. Together with two Renault FT-17 tanks delivered by the Finns, they would form an armored division in the White Army engaged in the conquest of Petrograd. The 6 Mark V Composite tanks were named: *"Brown Bear"*, *"Brown Bear"* II, *"Capt. Cromie"*, *"Deliverance"*, *"First Aid"* and *"White Soldier"*.

The Mark V tanks entered combat at the end of September, still manned by a British crew, as the training of Russian tank drivers had not been completed.

At the end of October the offensive to conquer Petrograd failed and the White Army troops were defeated and forced to retreat. The Mark V tanks were saved from capture by the Red Army and transported to Estonia by rail. Four were given to the Estonian Army and two to the Latvian Army. The two FT-17s were given back to Finland in April 1920.

The four British Mark V Composite tanks delivered to the Estonian Army were:
- 9018 *"Capt. Cromie"* - renamed *"Päälik"* by the Estonians
- 9349 *"Brown Bear"* - renamed *"Vahtula"* by the Estonians
- 9147 *"White Soldier"* - renamed by Estonians *"UKU"*.
- 9261 *"First Aid"* - renamed by the Estonians as *"Valdaja"*.

The Uku and *"Valdaja"* wagons had the 57 mm gun positioned in the left sponson and the machine guns in the right sponson, while the *"Päälik"* and *"Vahtula"* wagons had the armament reversed, the gun on the right and the machine guns on the left.

With Service Order No. 770 of 26 November 1919, issued by Commander-in-Chief General Laidoner, Captain Hans Vanaveski was commissioned to organize a training unit for the new unit equipped with Mark V tanks. The establishment of the new unit was approved on November 23 by the Minister of War. Shortly before the end of the War of Independence, two tanks named *"Puuk"* and *"Sorts"* were added to the Soomusautode Kolonn, the first armed with a 57 mm cannon and the second with a 76 mm anti-aircraft cannon. The battery was completed by an ammunition transport truck on the chassis of the American TAD 3-ton truck and two 76 mm field guns mod. 1902.

With the end of the war the Soomusautode Kolonn underwent a reorganization with the establishment of five operational groups:
- Group 1: armored cars *"Kalevipoeg"*, *"Pisuhänd"*, *"Estonia"*
- Group 2: armored cars *"Wibaune"*, *"Toonela"*, *"Wahur"*
- Group 3: armored cars *"Tasuja"*, *"Kotkasilm"*, *"Erilane"*/ *"Lembit"*
- Group 4: armored cars *"Suur Tõll"*, *"Wambola"*
- Artillery group: armored vehicles *"Puuk"*, *"Sorts"*

In addition to the armored vehicles included in the groups there were: 6 heavy trucks, 2 light trucks, 1 ammunition transport truck, 1 car and 4 motorcycles. Among the armored vehicles in the

---

5 The British Mark V tank had entered service in 1918, the Male version was armed with 2 Ordnance QF 6 lb 57 mm guns and 4 Hotchkiss Mle 1909 7.7 mm machine guns, the Female version was armed with 6 Hotchkiss Mle 1909 7.7 mm machine guns, the Composite version, also called Hermaphrodite, was armed with 1 Ordnance QF 6 lb 57 mm cannon and 3 Hotchkiss Mle 1909 7.7 mm machine guns.

group there was also the armored car *"Vanapagan"* that, since it was never homologated, was used only for training purposes for some years and then stored waiting to be demolished.

In 1920 12 Renault FT-17 tanks were ordered from France, 4 armed with the Hotchkiss 37 mm gun and the other 8 with the Hotchkiss Mle 1914 8 mm machine gun.

On 1 February 1921 the Soomusrongide Divisjon was transformed into Soomusrongide Brigaad, Armored Brigade, without changing the size of the departments of its staff.

On August 1, 1923 the Soomusrongide Brigade underwent a new reorganization, the 1st armored train regiment (1st Soomusrongirügemement), stationed in Tapa, and the 2nd armored train regiment (2nd Soomusrongirügement) stationed in Valga, while the armored and armored vehicles were merged into the new Auto-tankdivisjion.

The only occasion in which the FT-17 tanks in service with the Estonian Army were involved was on 1 December 1924, during an attempted coup d'état organized by the Comintern in Tallinn. A group of 30 rioters had the task of conquering the barracks where the FT-17 tank company was quartered and convincing the soldiers to join them.

Entering the barracks, with the help of a NCO of the Auto-tankdivisjion, the group of insurgents managed to take possession of the garage where the 12 tanks were parked. After realizing that only the NCO was able to drive one tank, the other 11 FT-17s were tampered with by cutting the electrical cables to prevent their use. The FT-17 driven by the non-commissioned officer, with a rioter at the machine gun, went towards the carriage gate with the intention of going out into the street and supporting the other groups of rioters engaged in the conquest of the institutional headquarters and other barracks.

Since the machine gun's ammunition had been removed shortly before the wagon's capture by a soldier loyal to the Republic, the wagon was practically unarmed and, after being blocked in front of the barracks' exit door, it was confronted by an officer who managed to kill the driver and recapture the wagon. Thus ended the attempt to use armored vehicles to support the communist uprising, which in a short time was overwhelmed.

The Ministry of War between 1924 and 1925 drew up a plan for the construction of a new light armored car to be built at the Arsenal arms factory in Tallinn. As there was no automobile industry in Estonia, the chassis and engine were ordered from the British factory Crossley Motors Ltd, while the armor plates were ordered from Sweden.

The assembly of the armored car was carried out at the Arsenal of Tallinn and the first vehicles were delivered to the Estonian army in 1926. The armored car was named Arsenal-Crossley or M27/28.

Between 1926 and 1928 a total of 13 armored cars were built, 6 armed with a 37 mm Hotchkiss gun in a rotating turret and the other 7 with a 7.7 mm Madsen machine gun. It was a 4x2 vehicle, armored with plates of varying thickness from 7 to 3 mm, with the interior floor covered with pine boards and the walls with felt and canvas for protection from shrapnel. The wheels were equipped with semi-pneumatics, the weight varied between 5.4 and 6.1 tons, the maximum speed was 60 km / h and the crew consisted of 4 soldiers.

At the time it was without any doubt the best vehicle in service in the Estonian army.

Of the 13 armored cars, two, armed with a 37mm cannon, were delivered to Kaitseliit, which put them into service, calling them *"Kõu"* and *"Pikker"*, remaining in charge until the Soviet invasion. The armored car platoon was part of the Malev (County Brigade) of Tallinn which, in 1930, was renamed Tallinna Maleva uksik soomusautoruhm (armored car platoon of the Malev of Tallinn).

With the other 11 armored cars, the armored car company was formed by 4 platoons, each consisting of one M27/28 armed with the gun and 2 M27/28 armed with the machine gun. Since there were only 7 available M27/28s with machine guns instead of the planned 8, the old *"Pisuhänd"* was used in one platoon for the second armored car with machine guns.

On 28 September 1928, following the reorganization of the Estonian Army, the Auto-tankdivisjion was transformed into Auto-Tank rügement, subordinate to the 3rd Division.

Its personnel was as follows:

- Headquarters (Tallinn)
- Training company in the barracks in Juhkentali street (Tallinn)
- Warehouse at the summer training area in Männiku (Tallinn)
- Light Tank Company in the barracks in Afrika street (Tallinn)
- Heavy Tank Group (Tallinn)
- Reserve armored car group (Tallinn)
- Car company in the barracks in Suurtüki street (Tallinn)
- 1st Armored Car Company - Tapa
    - Group 1: *"Kotkasilm"*, *"Tasuja"*, *"Wibuane"* in Narva
    - Group 2: *"Lembit"*, *"Suur Tõll"*, *"Pisuhänd"*, *"Vambola"* in Tapa
- 2nd Armored Car Company: Arsenal-Crossley M27/28 armored car – Valga

The available vehicles were: 22 old and new armored cars, 12 FT-17 light tanks and 4 Mark V Composite heavy tanks.

In 1934, due to its obsolescence, the armored car *"Vanapagan"* was cancelled and deleted from the records of the reserve armored car group.

In 1934 6 TKS tankettes were purchased from Poland and delivered on February 7, 1935, to form the 3rd company quartered in Tallinn.

With the arrival of the TKS tankettes in the course of 1935, a reorganization of the Auto-Tank Rügement was decided. The facilities were efficient and modern, the training was good, but the vehicles were outdated and obsolete. The four Mark V Composite tanks were removed from the rolls and put in a warehouse, the available vehicles were divided into 3 mixed companies and the regiment assumed the following structure:

- 1st Company: 9 armored cars M1918/19 and Arsenal-Crossley (Tallinn)
- 2nd Company: 3 FT-17 tanks and 9 Arsenal-Crossley armored cars (Tartu)
- 3rd Company: 9 FT-17 tanks and 6 TKS tankettes (Tallinn)

During the Defense Council meeting held at the end of 1935, Major General Nikolai Reek declared that only the Arsenal-Crossley armored cars and the TKS tankettes were capable of fighting in the defense of Estonia, since the FT-17 tanks, the Independence War armored cars and the Mark V Composite tanks were obsolete and of little or no war value.

The lack of funds prevented the programming of a modernization plan to purchase new vehicles and to update those considered still valid. It was only in 1939 that a modernization plan for the vehicles in service was drawn up, which foresaw for the Arsenal-Crossley to standardize the armament of all 11 armored cars with a 37 mm semi-automatic gun in the turret and a 7.7 mm Madsen machine gun mounted in front of the driver's side, as well as a Suomi machine gun for the crew. Lack of funding first, then the subsequent Soviet invasion, however, did not allow any upgrades to the Arsenal-Crossleys.

In order to strengthen the police force of the capital Tallinn, in function of anti-guerrilla warfare against possible communist revolts, in 1936 was purchased from Sweden an L-180 Landswerk armored car, armed with a 20 mm Madsen cannon and two MG machine guns. The armored car was delivered in 1937.

At the beginning of 1940, the Auto-Tank Rügement underwent yet another reorganization, with the elimination of the 3rd Company, whose vehicles went to reinforce both the 1st and 2nd Companies.

The Soviet invasion took place on June 16, 1940 with the army and the Kaitseliit which, with a few rare exceptions, obeyed the instructions given by the Estonian government and surrendered without resistance to the Red Army troops. In the following days, the vehicles in charge of the Auto-Tank ranks were massed at the training camp of Männiku, from where they were later sorted by order of the Soviets. The Auto-Tank gathering was abolished at the end of September 1940.

The destiny of the vehicles captured by the Soviets was varied, it appears that the TKS and Arsenal-Crossley entered into service with the newly formed Estonian 22nd Territorial Rifle Corps in service with the Red Army, with some vehicles assigned to the 180th Reconnaissance Battalion.

Four FT-17 tanks were transferred to Daugavpils in Latvia, at unit 2193, while the other 8 were sent to Bauska in Latvia at unit 2208. Their subsequent fate is unknown, although they were probably sent to the Soviet Union, along with the old armored cars of the War of Independence, to be demolished for steel, although it would appear that some FT-17s were buried and used as machine gun emplacements.

The Arsenal-Crossley M27/28 *"Kõu"* in Kaitseliit service was shipped to the 942nd Depot in Daugavpils and its end is unknown. In a German news film an Arsenal-Crossley can be seen burnt along the road leading to the city of Paldiski after its capture by German troops, but it is not clear whether it is the *"Kõu"* or one of the other armored cars captured by the Soviets and then used in the first phase of the Nazi invasion.

The fate of the 4 Mark V Composite tanks stored in a barracks in Tallinn and then assigned to the Baltic Special Military District was different. In August 1941, when the German troops were about to attack Tallinn, the four old Mark V Composite tanks were reused by the Soviets as forts and positioned in the suburbs of the city, along the line of fire on the Pirita river, armed with Maxim machine guns and 45 mm cannons. Of course their contribution to the defense of Tallinn was less than mediocre, but nevertheless more than 22 years after their arrival in Estonia they were still involved in combat, their last combat!

With the fighting in defense of the capital Tallinn by the old Mark V Composite ended the history of the Estonian armored units, which began in 1919. After regaining independence in 1991, and restoring the armed forces, the new Eesti Maavägi currently has no armored vehicles in service but only infantry fighting vehicles.

▲ The armored car *"Pisuhänd"* during the War of Independence.

CAMOUFLAGE, INSIGNIA, REGISTRATION NUMBER

Identifying the colors of the camouflage of the vehicles in service in the Eesti Maavägi in the early years of its establishment is not easy, even the photographs, in black and white, help very little to define the colors correctly.

The Mark V Composite tanks, after being delivered by the British, were painted in uniform dark green, while the FT-17s were delivered from France some in uniform dark green and some in camouflage. In the 1920's all were painted in dark green uniform.

The Arsenal-Crossley were painted in dark green uniform while the TKS remained in service with the original Polish camouflage of the first type in three colors: yellowish sand, olive green and gray-blue, with the profiles of the colors edged with a thin black line. According to other sources, instead of blue-gray, the color was dark brown and the sand was a lighter shade.

The armored cars used during the war of independence were initially painted in a uniform dark green, then some received a camouflage with spots probably dark brown and yellow sand on the dark green background. In the '20s they were camouflaged with large green stripes on a yellow sand or light ochre background, the stripes had the edges surrounded by a thick line of dark brown.

In winter, the vehicles were usually camouflaged using washable white paint, in some cases completely, see the TKS, in others, see the armored cars of the War of Independence, in spots with sharp edges.

All armored and armored vehicles in service in the Estonian Army never had insignia painted on the vehicles or even tactical symbols, only in some cases, during demonstrations or exercises, a small Estonian flag was carried on a pole attached to the turret.

The Mark V Composite tanks do not appear to have received an identification number, only the name painted on the sides and bow. The names were Uku, *"Päälik"*, *"Vahtula"* and *"Valdaja"*.

The Renault FT-17 tanks did not receive names but an identification number, only No 52 and No 57 are known with certainty. Most likely the numbering should be from 50 to 61. In the early '20s the number was placed on the sides of the vehicle under the initials A.T.D. the acronym of Auto-tankdivisjion, an acronym that disappeared in the '30s, since since 1928 the Auto-tankdivisjion had been replaced by the Auto-Tank rügement.

The six TKS tankettes were also not given names, but received the following numbers: 153, 156, 158, 159, 164 and 165.

The 11 Arsenal-Crossleys in service in the Eesti Maavägi were not given names, but were identified with the numbers: 141, 142, 143, 144, 145, 146, 147, 148, 149, 150 and 151. The two armored cars in service in the Kaitseliit were instead named *"Kõu"* and *"Pikker"* without any numbers.

The armored cars built during the War of Independence were always marked with a name painted on the sides of the vehicle. These are the names assigned to the 9 armored cars in service: Estonia, *"Vanapagan"*, *"Kotkasilm"*, *"Tasuja"*, *"Wibaune"*, *"Lembit"*, *"Suur Tõll"*, *"Pisuhänd"*, *"Vambola"*, remembering that another armored car lost had the name *"Tasuja"* and that the *"Lembit"* was originally called *"Erilane"*. Around 1930 on some armored cars an identification number appeared on the front armor of the vehicle, we know of n. 129 for the *"Wibaune"* and n. 126 for the *"Kotkasilm"*.

The two armored cars had no identification number but were marked with the names *"Puuk"* and *"Sorts"*.

▲ The armored cars "*Kotkasilm*" and "*Wibaune*" with their crews in 1932

▼ Armored car "*Vanapagan*" with its crew during the War of Independence in July 1919.

► The armored car "*Tasuja*" on January 1, 1926 in the courtyard of the Narva Fortress.

▲ The armored car “*Lembit*”, originally named “*Erilane*”, at the head of an armored column.

▲ The car fleet of the Auto-Tank Division in the camp in the summer of 1924. The armored cars “Suur-Tõll”, “*Tasuja*”, “*Wambola*” and another unidentified one are present.

◄ The armored car “*Kotkasilm*” on January 1, 1926 in the courtyard of the Narva Fortress.

▲ The Mark V Composite "*Vahtula*" tank parades during an event in the summer of 1925.

▶ A Mark V Composite tank parades through the streets of Tallinn in 1920.

▼ The armored car "*Tasuja*" and an armored car Arsenal-Crossley in the streets of Narva in winter 1930.

▲ Mark V tanks, Renault FT-17 and armored cars during a demonstration at the end of the War of Independence.

▼ The armored car *"Toonela"*

▲ The armored car *"Kalevipoeg"* with the crew in Võru in 1919.

▼ *British Mark V Composite tank No. 9261, prior to delivery to Estonian military authorities, at Narva on Nov. 25, 1919*

▲ British tank training officer from Estonia, Captain Frederick Edwin Alfred Manning , in front of Mark V Composite Tank No. 9147.

▼ The Fiat-Izhorsky armored car *"Wambola"* during an exercise in the mid '20s

▲ Mark V Composite "*UKU*" and "*VAHTULA*" tanks during the parade on February 24, 1925.

▼ A Mark V Composite tank of the Estonian Defense Forces drives along the Pärnu Road in Tallinn in the spring of 1920.

▼ Demonstration of the Mark V Composite tank's operational capabilities on a Tallinn beach in 1920.

▲ Demonstration of the Mark V Composite tank's operational capabilities on a Tallinn beach in 1920.

▶ Tankers and mechanics engaged in the repair of Mark V Composite tank 9349.

▼ The Mark V Composite *"UKU"* tank, followed by three other Mark V Composites and FT-17s, returns to the barracks after a parade on November 22, 1926.

◄ A Mark V Composite tank used by the Soviets in the defense of Tallinn in August 1941 and captured by the Germans.

▼ Two Mark V Composite tanks and an FT-17 in the barracks in the early 1920s.

▼ Six FT-17 tanks during training.

▲ Renault FT-17 tank during a phase of training.

▼ All 12 Renault FT-17 tanks deployed in 1920 shortly after entering service.

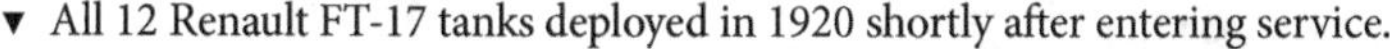

▲ Tank Regiment infantrymen in front of an FT-17 in the winter of 1936.

▼ A group of FT-17 tanks waiting to begin training.

▲ Renault FT-17 tanks and Arsenal-Crossley armored cars deployed at the 3rd anniversary of the birth of the Armored Division on November 22, 1926 in Tallinn.

◄ FT-17 tank during training.

▼ FT-17 tanks during maneuvers at Otepää in 1925.

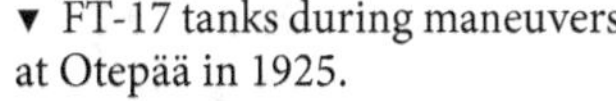

▲ FT-17 tanks with their crews during a parade in Tallinn in the 1930s (from "Tankai Lietuvos kariuomenėje 1924-1940 m.," op. cit. in bibliography).

▼ FT-17 tank during training.

▼ Photographic sequence relating to the crossing of an anti-tank ditch by an FT-17 tank equipped with an experimental system for laying two beams to allow the tank to pass over them.

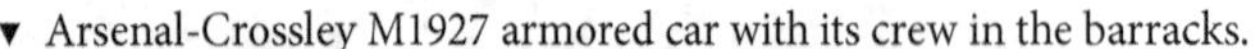

▲ FT-17 tanks and Arsenal-Crossley armored cars at maneuvers in 1935.

▼ Arsenal-Crossley M1927 armored car with its crew in the barracks.

▲ Arsenal-Crossley armored car No. 144 with its crew in the barracks.

▼ Arsenal-Crossley armored cars No. 149 and 144 during an exercise.

▲ Arsenal-Crossley armored cars No. 149 and 148 in the barracks.
▼ Six Arsenal-Crossley M27/28 armored cars during an exercise in the 1930s.

▼ Arsenal-Crossley armored cars transported on a railroad convoy in 1935.

▲ Arsenal-Crossley M27/28 No. 150 armored car poised on a moving bridge for a mobility experiment.
▼ Arsenal-Crossley M27/28 "*Pikker*" and "*Kõu*" armored cars in service in the "Kaitseliit ", the Estonian Defense League.

▼ Arsenal-Crossley armored cars "*Pikker*" and "*Kõu*" along with two other armored cars during a winter exercise.

▲ M27/28 armored cars (in the background) and Polish TKS tankettes waiting to begin exercises.

▼ Arsenal-Crossley M27/28 and old armored cars modernized and camouflaged during maneuvers at Valdeku field in 1932.

▲ Presentation of the TKS tankette to the Estonian Army in 1934.

▼ Estonian recruits beside a TKS tankette in a barracks in 1935 (from "Tankai Lietuvos kariuomenėje 1924-1940 m.," op. cit. in bibliography).

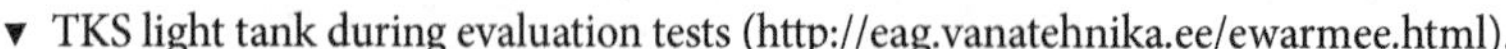

▲ Tankette TKS in front of the Armored Regiment Headquarters in the winter of 1937 (from "Tankai Lietuvos kariuo-menėje 1924-1940 m.," op. cit. in bibliography).

▼ TKS light tank during evaluation tests (http://eag.vanatehnika.ee/ewarmee.html).

▲ TKS light tank during evaluation tests (http://eag.vanatehnika.ee/ewarmee.html).

▼ Tankers of the Arsenal-Crossley and TKS armored cars consume ration during winter maneuvers mel 1937 (from "Tankai Lietuvos kariuomenėje 1924-1940 m.," op. cit. in bibliography).

▲ TKS tankettes deployed prior to the start of exercises in 1936.

▼ The autocannon *"Sortsi"*, equipped with 76 mm Putilov cannon, belonging to the Auto-Tank Division during a ceremony in Tallinn in 1928.

▼ Armored car *"Landsverk"* L180 in service with Tallinn Police.

▲ The truck *"Sortsi"* in barracks in Tallinn.

▼ The armored car Arsenal-Crossley M27/28 *"Pikker"* in service in the "Kaitseliit ", the Estonian Defense League.

▲ TKS 153 tankette during an exercise in 1936.

▼ Renault FT-17 tanks transported on railroad cars in the late 1920s.

▲ A platoon of Renault FT-17 tanks during summer maneuvers at the Nursipalu firing range on August 30, 1930.

▲ The reconstructed armored car *"Estonia"* parades in front of the authorities during the ceremony for the anniversary of independence

▼ The six TKS tankettes in training in 1939.

▲ TKS 165 tankette during an exercise in 1936.

▼ Arsenal-Crossley M27/28 armored cars belonging to the Auto-Tank Rügement with their crews in the barracks.

ARMOURED UNITS OF LATVIA

The first armored cars present in Latvia at the end of 1918 were not vehicles of the newly formed Republic, but three vehicles in service with the Latvian Fusiliers of the Latvian 1st Soviet Division. It was a small unit formed by the armed cars *"Imanta"*, *"Lāčplēsis"* and *"Komūnists*[6]*".* under the orders of commander Kaugurs, which were little used because of the constant breakdowns that forced them to continuous repairs, made difficult by the scarcity of spare parts.

The new government of Latvia, born as a result of the declaration of independence of November 18, 1918, initially could only count on a few hundred soldiers able to oppose the thousands of men of the Red Army, equipped only with a few light weapons, a few cannons and no armored vehicles. When in May 1919, with the help of German troops, Riga was liberated, were found some armored cars abandoned by the Bolshevik units that, initially, were used by the Baltische Landeswehr but, after the defeat suffered by the Germans in Cēsis in June 1919 by Estonian and Latvian troops, were later incorporated into the Latvian army.

In June 1919 the armored cars *"Lāčplēsis"* and *"Zemgalietis"* supported the Latvian units during the fights against the Bolsheviks in the area of Krustpils and Līvāni.

On July 10, 1919, thanks to the military successes obtained on the northern and southern fronts, and the liberation of the capital Riga, it was possible to unite the troops of the 1st Southern Latvian Brigade with those of the Northern Latvian Brigade, thus beginning the organization of the Latvian army.

On July 12 the 1st Army Division[7] of the Latvian Army was formed, which included armed trains, armed cars and later also tanks, and approved the organization chart of the structure and personnel of the Armed Car Division. It was planned to form 2 armored car divisions: one with light vehicles and one with heavy vehicles, with a total of 40 soldiers.

On 14 July 1919, under the command of Captain Otto Grossbart, the formation of the 1st and 2nd Armored Car Division began at the barracks of 77 Nikolaja Street in Riga.

The armored cars in service in the Latvian army at that date were four:

- Armored car Sheffield - Simplex *"Imanta"*
- 2 Garford-Putilov M1916 armored cars *"Lachplēsis"* and *"Kurzemnieks*[8]*".*
- Austin-Putilov armored car 2nd series *"Zemgalietis"*[9]*".*

On August 14, a motorcycle company was formed.

While the constitution of the new units and the training of the military proceeded, a new front of war opened, this time not against the Bolsheviks but against the Germans and the Russians under the command of the Russian general Pavel Bermondt-Avalov. The short war was also called Bermontiade from the name of the general who commanded the Russian-German army.

At the beginning of October, the 1st Division had 3 armored cars ready for combat: *"Kurzemnieks"*, *"Zemgalietis"*, *"Lāčplēsis"* and 2 in repair, *"Imanta"* and *"Staburags*[10]*",* as well as a discrete number of

---

6 The armored car *"Imanta"* was a Sheffield - Simplex, the *"Lāčplēsis"* was a Garford-Putilov M1916, the brand of the *"Komūnists"* is unknown, it could have been a Fiat-Izhorski or an Austin-Putilov.

7 The term Division in this case should not be understood as a large military unit, but as the basic military unit of the self-armored department. By the consistency of vehicles and personnel it is comparable to the force normally in charge of a Platoon.

8 In the examined documentation is always described the presence of two armored cars Garford-Putilov, but according to some sources instead was only one vehicle in service in the Latvian army, the *"Lāčplēsis"*, which when it was captured by the Germans, reused and then given to the Latvians after the defeat, was renamed *"Kurzemnieks"*.

9 This may be the *"Komūnists"* armored car captured from the Soviets in late 1918 and renamed *"Zemgalietis"*.

10 The *"Staburags"* armored car was a Fiat-Izhorski captured from the Red Army in poor condition, repaired and used until 1940.

trucks and cars, used for supplies and connections, and motorcycles. Although difficulties remained for the maintenance of vehicles, due to the scarcity of spare parts and weapons, the division was actively used in combat.

In October and November 1919, the armored cars *"Lāčplēsis"*, *"Kurzemnieks"*, *"Zemgalietis"* and *"Imanta"* supported the infantry units engaged in battles against General Bermondt's troops in the districts of Jelgava, Kalnciems, Smārde and Tukums, also damaging 3 enemy armored trains.

On October 8 the *"Lāčplēsis"*, while reversing at low speed under an enemy counterattack on the Jelgava highway near the cemetery of Baloži, was attacked by a German officer who shot dead the driver and the commander of the armored car. The vehicle fell into a ditch and was then captured by the Germans who, after recovering it, used it again.

The armored cars *"Kurzemnieks"* and *"Zemgalietis"* were employed in the defense of the Dauga-va bridge in Riga. On the night of 4-5 November, *"Imanta"* and *"Kurzemnieks"* were moved to the left bank of the Daugava in the Bolderāja district. On November 10 *"Kurzemnieks"* supported the offensive of the 9th Rezekne Regiment that liberated Bulduri, being damaged during the fight and replaced in the continuation of the attack by *"Zemgalietis"*.

After the liberation of Riga on November 11, the activity of the autoblidades continued to defeat the retreating troops of Bermondt and to free the whole Latvian territory from the invaders. The retreating enemy left a substantial booty of weapons and vehicles in the hands of Latvian soldiers, including an armored car and two autocannons.

They were an Izhorsky-Pierce-Arrow armored car called *"Titanic"*, armed with a 76 mm M1904 mountain gun and two Maxim machine guns in the rear of the vehicle, and renamed *"Viesturs"* and two Daimler-Krupp BAK Kw 14, trucks armed with a 75 mm anti-aircraft gun, called *"Max"* and *"Moritz"* by the Germans, which the Latvians renamed *"Pērkons"* and *"Tālivaldis"*. The *"Staburags"* were immediately redeployed by their new owners and sent to the front from 18 November.

The *"Imanta"* took part in the battle near Smārde on 19 November, where she was captured by the enemy and recovered on the 22nd.

The eastern region of Latgale still remained in enemy hands. The Latvian army, driven by the success obtained with the liberation of the capital Riga and the defeat of the Bermontians, continued its offensive, despite the cease-fire requested by the enemy. In the operations in Latgale *"Tālivaldis"*, *"Staburags"*, *"Zemgalietis"* and *"Kurzemnieks"* had a relevant weight in the battles against the Bol-sheviks.

Following the defeat of General Judenich's White Army, a number of British tanks were available at the time deployed in Tallinn. At the beginning of December 1919 two Mark V Composite tanks were purchased followed by another Mark V Composite and two Mark B tanks[11].

With the five new tanks, a tank battalion was formed in the 1st Army Division.

The tanks, when taken over, received the following name::

- Mark V Tank No. 9116 - *"Ministr. Pres. Ulmanis"* in honor of the Prime Minister
- Tank Mark V n° 9369 - *"Generalis Balodis"* in honor of General Balodis
- Tank Mark V n° 9147 - *"Generalis Burt's"* in honor of the English General Alfred Bert
- Mark B Tank n° 1209 - *"Latgalietis"*.
- Tank Mark B n° 1615 - *"Vidzemnieks"*.

They did not participate in the last stages of the War of Independence, but were deployed in the Daugavpils area for protection.

On December 12, 1919 the reorganization of the 1st Army Division concerning the component of

---

11 The British Medium Mark B tank was developed as a successor to the Whippet, but due to the end of the war, as well as problems encountered during its entry into service, it was built in only 102 units, of which only 45 entered service. It was armed with 4 Hotchkiss Mle 1909 7.7 mm machine guns with the possibility of positioning them in 7 ball joints located in the turret and on the flanks.

armored cars and tanks was approved. The new organization was implemented in January 1920 and as of February 1, the organization chart was as follows:

- Armored Car Company:
  - 1st armored car platoon: *"Kurzemnieks"*, *"Zemgalietis"* and *"Lāčplēsis"*, 52 soldiers under the command of Lieutenant Georgs Dzeguze
  - 2nd Tank Platoon: *"Viesturs"*, *"Imanta"* and *"Staburags"*, 52 soldiers under the command   of Captain Aleksandrs Kaugars
- Tank Battalion - 3 Mark V and 2 Mark B tanks
- Motorcycle Company
- Tank Battery - *"Pērkons"* and *"Tālivaldis"*
- Training Company - 2 platoons, 1 armored car.

On February 8, 1920 the 1st Army Division was abolished and three autonomous Divisions were created in its place:

- Armored Car Division under the command of Lieutenant Colonel A. Paulock
- Armored Train Division under the command of Lieutenant J. Laveniek
- Tank Division under the command of Lieutenant Colonel P. Brunenieks

On 16 January 1922 the *Latvijas Tehniskā divīzija* - Latvian Technical Division was formed, which included:

- Engineer Regiment
- Tank Regiment (Autotank Regiment)
- Communications Battalion
- Armored Train Regiment
- Coastal Artillery Regiment

At the command of the new unit was appointed General Janis Kourelis.

In September 1925 6 Fiat 3000 Mod. 21 light tanks were purchased from Italy, two armed with 37mm Puteaux cannon and the other four with 7.7mm Vickers machine guns. The new tanks, delivered in early 1927, formed two platoons, each consisting of one tank with a gun and two with a machine gun, which were included in the tank battalion of the Autotank Regiment.

In 1926 there were 5 armored cars available in the Autotank Company, divided into 3 platoons:

- Command Platoon: *"Staburags"*
- Armored car platoon with cannon: *"Kurzemnieks"* and *"Viesturs"*
- Armored car platoon with machine guns: *"Zemgalietis"* and *"Imanta"*

Since it was necessary to integrate a new armored car into the command platoon and the defense budget had no funds, the population was asked for help. The Latvian Automobile Club - Latvijas Republikas Auto Klubs collected the necessary funds for the purchase of a FIAT truck chassis and armor from the English company Beardmore. When the materials were delivered the assembly of the new armored car was carried out at the workshop of the Tank Regiment-Auto-tanku pulka darbnīcās. The new armored car, armed with 7.7 mm Vickers machine guns, was officially delivered to the army on September 22, 1926, during a ceremony held in Esplanade Square in Riga with the participation of the President of the Republic, Jānis Čakste, and received the name *"Sargs"*.

In 1930, for the training of soldiers destined to the armored car company, an armored car was built based on the chassis of the Ford Model AA truck with a single turret.

In the same year the "Jelgava" Regiment of the Aizsargu organizācija-Organization of Guards, Latvian paramilitary corps, purchased a Carden Loyd Mark VI tankette, used in 1934 during the coup d'état to carry out patrols in the capital.

As the Latvijas Bruņotie spēki-Latvian Armed Forces realized the obsolescence of the vehicles in service with the Autotank Regiment, in 1935 the purchase of 12 Vickers Model 1936 light tanks equipped with a Vickers .303 machine gun and 6 Vickers Model 1937 tanks armed with an Ordnance QF 2-pounder 40 mm gun was approved. The M.1936 tanks were delivered on March 3, 1936 and the M.1937s on May 16, 1938. With the arrival of the Vickers tanks it was possible to establish two new tank companies, each consisting of 3 M.1937 tanks armed with cannon and 6 M.1936 tanks with machine guns. In 1938 was implemented the reorganization of the *Latvijas Tehniskā divīzija* - Latvian Technical Division, which was divided into autonomous regiments.

The Autotank Regiment was structured as follows:

- Autotank Company: "*Staburags*", "*Sargs*", "*Kurzemnieks*", "*Viesturs*", "*Zemgalietis*", "*Imanta*"
- 1st Company: Mark V, Mark B and Fiat 3000 tanks
- 2nd Company: Vickers M.1936/1937 tanks
- 3rd Company: tanks Vickers M.1936/1937
- Transport Company
- Training Company: Ford Model AA armored cars

The situation of the armored cars in service was rather precarious, they were vehicles with twenty years of service, repaired several times but never submitted to a radical overhaul that would eliminate the increasingly frequent problems due to old and worn engines and chassis. If in the mid '20s an intervention was carried out on the "*Kurzemnieks*", replacing the original engine with a new Wisconsin unit, it was in the mid '30s that began the work of reconditioning of the old armored cars, work carried out at the Auto-tanku pulka darbnīcās.

It began with the "*Zemgalietis*", whose armor was transferred on the chassis of a Fordson V8 truck purchased in Denmark, then in 1938 it was the turn of the "*Sargs*", where the old Fiat chassis was replaced with a Ford V8 chassis, while at the beginning of 1940 the "*Imanta*" was replaced with the original chassis of a Ford-Vairogs 91-T truck. Also in 1940 it was planned to replace the old chassis of the "*Staburags*" with that of a Ford-Vairogs 91-T, but the Soviet invasion blocked the work.

On September 1, 1939 the Autotank Regiment had a staff of 35 officers, 274 non-commissioned officers and graduates, 515 soldiers and 21 civilians and was structured on:

- Armored car company stationed in Riga
  - Command Platoon: "*Staburags*" and "*Sargs*"
  - Armored platoon with cannon: "*Kurzemnieks*"[12] and "*Viesturs*"
  - Armored platoon with machine guns: "*Zemgalietis*" and "*Imanta*"
- 1st Tank Company stationed in Riga
  - 1st platoon: 2 Mark V tanks and 1 Mark B tank
  - 2nd platoon: 1 Fiat 3000 armed with cannon and 2 Fiat 3000 armed with machine guns
  - 3rd platoon: 1 Fiat 3000 armed with cannon and 2 Fiat 3000 armed with machine guns
- 2nd Tank Company deployed in Daugavpils[13]
  - 1st platoon: 1 Vickers M.1936 and 2 Vickers M.1937
  - 2nd platoon: 1 Vickers M.1936 and 2 Vickers M.1937
  - 3rd platoon: 1 Vickers M.1936 and 2 Vickers M.1937
- 3rd Tank Company stationed in Riga
  - 1st platoon: 1 Vickers M.1936 and 2 Vickers M.1937
  - 2nd platoon: 1 Vickers M.1936 and 2 Vickers M.1937
  - 3rd platoon: 1 Vickers M.1936 and 2 Vickers M.1937
  - Transport Company
- Truck platoon: 12 Albion heavy trucks
- Truck Platoon: 18 medium trucks Ford-Vairogs V8-51

12 The presence of the "*Kurzemnieks*" in service in September 1939 is very doubtful, according to some sources the armored car had already been taken out of service in the early 1930s. It is very likely that it had been shelved in the barracks and not removed from the registration records.
13 According to another source the 2nd Company was in Riga and the 3rd in Daugavpils.

- Training Company: Ford Model AA armored car, Mark C or B tank, light tank[14]

The total number of vehicles in service in the regiment was: 27 tanks, 6 tank trailers, 6 armored cars, 30 trucks, 10 passenger cars, and 15 motorcycles. At the end of 1939 only two Mark V Composite tanks were still a service, the other 3 Mark V and B tanks had been sent for scrapping.

On October 5, 1939 the Latvian government was forced to sign a cooperation pact with the Soviet Union, which included, among other clauses, the obligation to purchase armaments only from Soviet industries and allowed the Soviets to establish military and naval bases on Latvian territory.

The leadership of Latvijas Bruņotie spēki, urged by the Government that had planned a substantial increase in the defense budget, began to draw up plans for the strengthening of the armored sector, showing considerable interest in the purchase of T-26 tanks and T-20 Komsomolec light tractors. These purchases did not materialize due to the subsequent Soviet invasion.

In the early months of 1940 the *Latvijas Tehniskā divīzija* was disbanded and on March 1 the Autotank Regiment was renamed Latvijas Autotanku brigade. The brigade was initially stationed in the barracks of Via Pulka in Riga, with a company deployed in Daugavpils near the defensive line prepared to face a possible Soviet invasion, but later the headquarters was transferred to Cēsis. The brigade was under the command of General Otto Grossbart who was replaced by Colonel Jānis Kaļķis.

On June 16, 1940 the Soviet Union sent an ultimatum to the Latvian government and on the 17th invaded Latvia. The occupation was peaceful, also because the Latvian Government had given instructions to Latvijas Bruņotie spēki not to react.

Following the Soviet invasion, all tanks and armored cars were requisitioned. The fate of the Mark V and B and the Fiat 3000 is unknown, although, given their obsolescence, it is presumable that they were scrapped, as well as the armored cars. Instead, the Vickers[15] tanks were assigned to the 23rd Armored Division of the 12th Mechanized Corps, a division composed only of Soviet soldiers, while Latvian soldiers became part of the 181st and 183rd Rifle Divisions of the 24th Territorial Rifle Corps.

The Latvijas Autotanku brigāde ceased to exist in July 1940.

---

14 The vehicles used by the Training Company were certainly the Ford Model AA armored car and probably a Mark V tank and not a Mark B, since at that date only 2/3 Mark V tanks should have remained in service. Regarding the presence of the light tank, the only possibility that a vehicle was actually present is that the Vickers tanks purchased were not 18, as those regularly in service in the 2nd and 3rd Companies, but rather 20, as cited by one source.

15 Of the 18 Vickers tanks captured by the Soviets, the 12 M1936s armed with a machine gun were not considered fit for combat and were stored, while one M1937 tank armed with the 40-gun was shipped to Kubinka, where it is still located in the Armored Vehicle Museum, and the other 5 were used in the fighting against German troops.

▲ The armored car Ižoras FIAT 55 *"Staburags"* at the closing parade of the maneuvers carried out in 1937.

CAMOUFLAGE, INSIGNIA, REGISTRATION NUMBER

The Mark V Composite and Mark B tanks were painted in uniform dark green, the Fiat 3000 had a three-color patch camouflage: yellow ochre, medium green and brown, outlined by a thin black line. The Carden Loyd Mk IV remained painted in olive green while the Vickers M1936 and M1937 were camouflaged with rust red and yellow ochre patches on a medium green base, the patches were surrounded by a thin black border. The armored cars were both in uniform olive green and camouflaged with sandy yellow, reddish brown, and light gray patches on an olive green base, with edges outlined by a black line. In the 1930s, the armored cars were repainted with three-color camouflage: olive green, sand yellow, and reddish brown. Between 1938 and 1939 they received a new repaint in uniform olive green.

On the Mark V Composite, Mark B, Fiat 3000 tanks and armored cars in service in the Autotanku brigāde there were never any insignia, only for the Vickers M 1936/1937 tanks an identification system was planned.

Since only the 12 machine gun tanks were in service in 1936, an initial codification of the identification system for the vehicles was made. The 2nd Company was identified with a white square and the 3rd Company with a white triangle. The 1st platoon of the 2nd company had a red circle inside the white square on the right side of the turret, the 2nd platoon had a red triangle inside the white square on the left side of the turret. The 1st platoon of the 3rd company had a red circle inside the white triangle on the left side of the turret and the 2nd platoon a red circle inside the white triangle on the right side of the turret.

In 1938, with the arrival of the other 6 Vickers tanks armed with 40 mm cannon, the 3rd platoon was constituted in each company, redistributing the tanks in service among the 6 platoons. In this way the identification system foreseen in the 1935 plan was fully implemented.

Therefore, in the 2nd company the 1st platoon was marked by a white square with a red circle in the middle positioned on the right side of the turret, the 2nd platoon by a white square with a red circle on the left side of the turret and the 3rd platoon by a white square with a red triangle on the left side of the turret.

In the 3rd Company, the 1st platoon by a white triangle with a red circle on the left side of the turret, the 2nd platoon by a white triangle with a red circle on the right side of the turret and the 3rd platoon by a white triangle with a red square on the right side of the turret.

During large parades a Latvian flag was hoisted on the turret of all vehicles.

Both Mark V Composite and Mark B tanks purchased from England initially retained the same British registration number, each receiving a name written under the inscription TANK DIVIS and two Latvian flags crossed on the flanks at the bow of the tank. The inscriptions were all in white. The names were *"Ministr. Pres. Ulmanis"* for tank 9116, *"Generalis Balodis"* for 9369 and *"Generalis Burt's "* for 9147. The two Mark B tanks were named *"Latgalietis"* the 1209 tank and *"Vidzemnieks"* the 1615. The Mark B tanks lacked the TANKU DIVIS inscription and flags, and the names were placed on the sides just after the centerline of the tank. In the 30's the TANKU DIVIS inscription, the crossed flags and the British registration number disappeared from the Mark V, and the inscriptions with the name of the wagon were reproduced on the sides of the bow but lower down. Also on the Mark B the British registration numbers were erased.

The Fiat 3000 tanks received the numbers 101 to 106 written in white on the sides under the turret. Tanks 101 to 103 formed the 1st platoon, 104 to 106 formed the 2nd platoon.

The Vickers M 1936/1937 tanks had the numbers 201 to 218, painted in white on a black background in the center of the tank bow and in white on the color of the tank on the back left (i.e. No. 201). Wagons 201 through 209 were in service in the 2nd Company, wagons 210 through 218 in the 3rd Company. The M.1937 tanks armed with cannon had the numbers 204 and 210 for sure and the numbers 201, 207, 213 and 216 almost certainly; the M.1936 had the numbers 202, 203, 205, 206, 208, 209, 211, 212 for sure and the numbers 214, 215, 217 and 218 almost certainly.

The armored cars did not have a registration number but each received a name: *"Imanta"*[16], *"Kurzemnieks"*, *"Zemgaleetis"*, *"Staburags"*, *"Viesturs"*, *"Lāčplēsis"*, *"Sargs"*, painted on the sides of the casemate in white. During the War of Independence, on the armored cars *"Zemgaleetis"* and *"Lāčplēsis"* were painted, as on the Mark V tanks, two crossed flags of Latvia above the inscription on both sides, above the flags there was an inscription in white which, however, could not be deciphered. On the armored cars *"Imanta"*, *"Staburags"*, and later also on the *"Zemgaleetis"*, instead there was a drawing where 2 wheels are represented connected by an axle on which are placed those that look very similar to the wings of Mercury with at the center at the top a circle surmounted by a stylized machine gun, with above a white writing not decipherable.

At the end of the war all the armored cars were repainted and appeared only more the white writing of the name on both sides.

The armored car *"Sargs"*, having been built with funds raised by the Automobile Club, had painted above the name the coat of arms of the Latvian Automobile Club[17].

---

16 A few years ago, at some farms in the municipality of Gulbene, dozens of parts of the armored car *"Imanta"* were recovered, including a machine gun tower, armor plates, axles, rims, etc.. etc.. Given the material impossibility, with the few pieces recovered, of fully reconstructing the *"Imanta"*, the Riga Motor Museum, using digital technologies, created a multimedia exhibition with which it was possible to virtually revive the armored vehicle.
17 The Latvian Automobile Club crest was later removed, probably in the early 1930s.

▲ The armored car Ižoras FIAT 55 *"Staburags"*.

▲ A group of armored cars parade through the streets of Riga on the occasion of the anniversary of the Declaration of Independence on November 18 in the early '20s, in the foreground the armored car Garford-Putilov "*Kurzemnieks*".

▼ The "*Sargs*"" armored car built on the chassis of a Fiat truck, donated by the Autoklub of the Republic of Latvia on September 22, 1926 to the Regiment on June 20, 1928.

▶ The Garford-Putilov armored car "*LACPLESIS*"" destroyed after the clashes of October 8, 1919.

▲ The armored car Ižoras Pierce-Arrow "*Viesturs*".

▼ An ex-Latvian Austin Mk.2 armored car at the head of the Soviet 24th Rifle Corps vehicle column in July 1941, destroyed during the early stages of the German invasion.

▲ The armored car Austin Mk.2 "*Zemgalietis*" in 1919, shortly after his entry into service in the ranks of the Latvian army.

▼ The armored car Austin Mk.2 "*Zemgalietis*" in the '30s after its reconstruction on the chassis Austin-Fordson V8.

▲ The Garford-Putilov armored car "*Kurzemnieks*" in the early 1920s.

▼ The Russian Garford-Putilov "*LACPLESIS*" armored car in service with Latvian forces in 1919 after its capture.

▲ The Sheffield-Simplex "*Jmanta*" armored car in 1928.

▼ The Mark V Composite tank "Minstr. Pres. Ulmanis" during an obstacle clearance demonstration.

▲ The Sheffield-Simplex *"Jmanta"* armored car, with its crew, after rebuilding on the new Ford-Shield chassis.

▼ Mark V Composite and Mark B armored cars and tanks during an exercise on July 14, 1928.

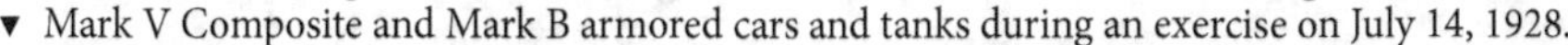

▼ The armored cars *"Jmanta"*, *"Viesturs"* and *"Kurzemnieks"* in the courtyard of the Riga barracks.

▲ The Sheffield-Simplex armored car captured from the Russians, renamed "*Imanta*", and immediately put into service in the Latvian armed forces.

▼ The armored car Garford-Putilov "*LACPLESIS*" in service in the Latvian units captured by the troops of General Bermont-Avalov in 1919.

▲ Latvian soldiers inspect the Panzerkraftwagen Krupp-Daimler 7.7cm FlaK "*Moritz*" captured on November 21, 1919 from the Germans of the Freikorps.

▼ The Panzerkraftwagen Krupp-Daimler 7.7cm FlaK "*Max*", in service in the German Freikorps, captured by the Latvians and reused in their units.

▲ Officers, non-commissioned officers and tankers in front of a Mark V and a Mark B.

▼ The Mark V Composite "Generalis Burt's" tank during training.

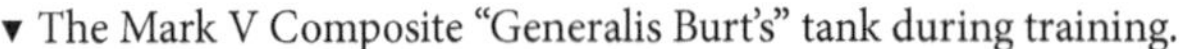

▲ The Mark V Composite tank "Generalis Balodis" engaged in overcoming obstacles during an exercise.

▼ In the foreground the Mark B *Latgalietis* tank, followed by the Mark V Composite *"Generalis Balodis"*, with their crews, at the Latvian Army military parade on the Esplanade in Riga in the early 1920s.

▼ The Mark V Composite tank *"Generalis Balodis"* engaged in overcoming obstacles in the barracks.

▲ The Mark V Composite tank *"Generalis Balodis"* loaded on a railroad flatbed surrounded by tankers in Riga.

▼ Mark B *"Latgalietis"* tanks during operations for loading on a railroad flatbed in Riga.

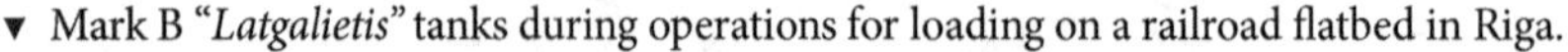

▲ The Mark V Composite tank *"Minstr. Pres. Ul-manis"* during a demonstration of overcoming fences.

► The tank Fiat 3000 No. 103 surrounded by tank drivers in the courtyard of the barracks.

▼ Carristians intent on the maintenance of the Mark B tank *"Latgalietis"*.

▲ The Fiat 3000 wagon n. 105 engaged in exercises carried out in 1928 together with another Fiat 3000 with an unidentified number.

▼ Fiat 3000 tanks, with crews, deployed at a celebration inside the Pulka Street Barracks in Riga in the early 1930s.

▼ Photograph of the armored car "*Sargs*", unfortunately of low quality, in which you can see the coat of arms of the Auto-klubs latvijas painted above the name of the vehicle. In small detail of the coat of arms.

▲ The six Fiat 3000 tanks deployed to begin maneuvers shortly after they entered service in the late 1920s.

▼ A Fiat 3000 tank surrounded by military personnel in barracks in 1926.

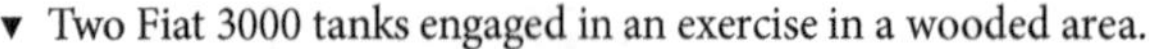

▲ All six Fiat 3000s on the march during an exercise on July 28, 1925.

▼ Two Fiat 3000 tanks engaged in an exercise in a wooded area.

▲ Motorcyclists and tankette Vichers-Carden Loyd Mk. VI of the National Guard in Market Square in Jelgava.

▼ Presentation of the Vickers-Carden Loyd Mark VI tankette to military authorities in Riga in 1930.

▲ Practice with the Vickers-Carden Loyd Mark VI tankette.

▼ Vickers M1936 tanks parade during a parade in Riga on May 15, 1936, tank No. 206 opens the column.

▲ Vickers M1936 and M1937 parade in Victory Square during the November 17, 1938 parade, led by float No. 212.

▼ LC Vickers M1936 tanks participate in the closing parade of the Tank Regiment maneuvers in 1937, led by tank No. 203.

▲ The crew of the Vickers M1936 No. 21 tank? in the courtyard of the Regimental barracks.

▼ Tankers around the Vickers M1936 No. 211 tank in the Regimental barracks.

▲ Vickers M1936 No. 214 tank, armed with a machine gun, during maneuvers in 1936.

▼ Infantrymen of the 2nd Company engaged in washing Vickers tanks in the Daugava at Daugavpils in 1937.

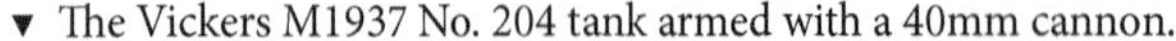

▲ Vickers M1936 tanks support cavalry divisions during maneuvers conducted in 1936.

▼ The Vickers M1937 No. 204 tank armed with a 40mm cannon.

▲ Vickers M1936 tanks during an exercise in the Ergļu area, in the foreground tank No. 209, in 1936.

▼ Vickers M1936 tanks on railroad flatbed ready for a move.

▲ Vickers M1937 and M1936 tanks marching for the November 18, 1937 parade in Daugavpils. Small photo: Tank Brigade chest badge.

◄ Latvian tankers deployed in the fortress of Daugavpils before beginning maneuvers in the winter of 1938.

▼ The Mark B *"Latgalietis"* tank another Mark B and a Mark V Composite deployed on Riga square at the end of maneuvers in the mid-1920s.

▼▼ Vickers M1936 tanks parade along Riga's Esplanades Square on May 15, 1937.

▲ Vickers M1937 tanks armed with 40mm cannon during winter training in 1939.

▼ Vickers M1937 tank armed with the 40mm cannon during an exercise in 1939, belongs to 3rd Platoon of 3rd Company.

▲ Soviet BT-7 tanks drive through the square in front of the station in Riga during the occupation of Latvia on June 17, 1940.

▼ A Soviet BT-7 tank, followed by a truck loaded with soldiers, drives through downtown Riga on June 17, 1940.

▲ Soviet tank BT-7 mod. 1937 destroyed in Vienibas Square in the city of Cesis in July 1941.

▲ Tankers and civilians pose for a photograph in front of three Vickers M1936 tanks during summer maneuvers in 1936.
▼ Maintenance to Vickers M1936 floats during summer maneuvers.

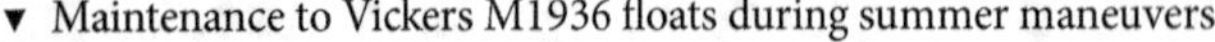

ARMORED UNITS OF LITHUANIA

Despite having declared its independence on February 16, 1918, until the month of November Lithuania remained occupied by German troops. The Red Army moved quickly, as soon as the German retreat began, quickly occupying the territory that remained without administration.

On November 23, 1918, the Minister of National Defense, Augustinas Voldemaras, issued an order establishing the Security Council and the formation of the first regiment of the Lithuanian armed forces. The newborn Lithuanian Army, *Lietuvos kariuomenės Sausumos pajėgos*, could count on a few hundred men, which increased to 3,000 volunteers in early March 1919, when compulsory conscription was ordered by Decree of March 5, 1919.

The difficulties encountered by the newly formed Lithuanian army were enormous, lacking weapons, not only cannons and heavy machine guns, but also rifles, pistols and ammunition, as well as the total absence of armored cars, tanks and armed trains.

In late May 1919 the first armored car was put into service. It was the Izhorsky-Fiat armored car No. 6739, armed with 2 Maxim 7.62 mm machine guns, in service with the 1st Infantry Regiment of the Red Army occupying the Ukmerge-Utena road in southern Lithuania.

Near the village of Klivėnai on May 31 the advance of Lithuanian troops, supported by German units, met with strong Bolshevik resistance. The Soviet units counter-attacked with infantry supported by artillery fire and an armored car.

The Lithuanian soldiers, belonging to the 2nd Infantry Regiment, retreated in an orderly fashion, hiding behind a hill. The Bolshevik armored car continued the pursuit of the Lithuanian soldiers without the support of the friendly infantry, so that when the road was blocked by felled trees, it was forced to stop and accept the fight. After a brief firefight the crew was forced to surrender and the armored car was captured. Having verified the good condition of the armored car, it was immediately reused and was named *"Žaibas»*, becoming the first armored vehicle of the *Lietuvos kariuomenės Sausumos pajėgos*.

In the last months of 1919, probably between November and December, the Lithuanian military captured in Radviliškis another armored car, this time in service in the army of General Bermondt, a "sonderwagen[18]" built by Ehrhardt. Immediately reused it was called *"Savanoris"*.

Between the end of 1919 and the beginning of 1920, following the defeat, the Germans were forced to withdraw from Lithuania abandoning the heavy war material. On 29 January 1920, at the railway station of Virbalis, the Lithuanian units took delivery of 4 armoured cars Ehrhardt-Behelfspanzerwagen[19] which, after being repaired, were reused.

The four armored cars taken over were given the following names:
- Ehrhardt-Behelfspanzerwagen No. 4010 - *"Sarunas"*.
- Ehrhardt-Behelfspanzerwagen No. 3992 - *"Perkunas"*.
- Ehrhardt-Behelfspanzerwagen No. 4004 - *"Aras"*
- Ehrhardt-Behelfspanzerwagen No. 4026 - *"PRAGARAS"*.

The four armored cars had some peculiarities that distinguished them from the *"Savanoris"*, which had entered service a few weeks earlier, although all five were Ehrhardt-Behelfspanzerwagen: the turret was square instead of round, they had no protection on the rear wheels, the engine hood and the front lights were different.

---

18 The sonderwagen were armored vehicles built on truck chassis and used by the German police during the Weimar Republic to maintain public order.

19 The armored cars Ehrhardt-Behelfspanzerwagen in many publications are written as Erhardt / Daimler Behelftswagen or as Daimler -Behelfspanzerwagen but this is not correct, because Erhardt and Daimler were two competing companies and never collaborated in the construction of an armored car.

With the six armoured cars in service on 1 March 1920 the *Šarvuočių rinktinė* - armoured platoon[20] - was formed in the Autobattalion - battalion car, which was engaged in the last battles against the Red Army in the spring and against the Poles in the area of Vilnius in the autumn. The staff consisted of 8 officers and 63 non-commissioned officers/graduates/soldiers, in addition to the 6 armored cars there were also 9 motor vehicles in service. There was no barracks dedicated to the department, but the officers and soldiers were housed in the homes of private citizens and the armored cars were parked outdoors.

Since the military leadership intended to establish armored units, but in Lithuania there were no tanks, agreements were made with neighboring Latvia to send Lithuanian soldiers at their training center. In March 1920 was sent to Riga a group of 13 officers and 45 soldiers to attend training courses for the use and maintenance of tanks.

At the end of the course, the soldiers returned to Lithuania, but since they still had no tanks in service, they were distributed among the various departments, thus dispersing all the professionalism acquired with considerable economic and personal efforts.

By secret order to the army no. 20 on August 1, 1921 the *Šarvuočių rinktinė* was transformed into the *Šarvuotasis autodivizionas* - Armored Car Division[21].

On January 8, 1922 the soldiers of the Division moved to the Žaliajame barracks, and on April 25, after installing and arranging the premises, the garages and transporting the armoured vehicles, they moved to the new barracks on Vytautas Hill.

Only in 1923, thanks to an improved economic situation, Lithuania purchased the first tanks, 12 Renault FT-17 that arrived in August. These were used tanks, veterans of the First World War, and in poor condition, some armed with cannon and others with machine guns. All FT-17s were repaired, repainted and rearmed with a German 7.92mm Maxin machine gun.

The tanks were stationed at the former Aukštoji Freda Manor, located in the Freda district of the Aleksotas municipality of Kaunas, where crew training began and ended on 17 May 1924 when the unit was declared operational.

Continuing the tradition established with the armoured cars, the FT-17s were also identified with a name: *"AUDRA"*, *"Kovas"*, *"Pagieža"*, *"Pikoulis"*, *"Drąsutis"*, *"Karžygys"*, *"Giltine"*, *"Kerštas"*, *"Slibinas"*, *"Galiūnas"*, *"Smūgis"*, *"GRIAUSTINIS"*.

In addition to the name the tanks received a new registration number with the inscription KAM (*Krašto Apsaugos Ministerija* - Ministry of Defence) followed by a number. For the FT-17 the plates were from KAM 1 to KAM 12.

In execution of the secret order to the Army No. 1 of 10 January 1924, the *Šarvuočių rinktinė* (Armored Squadron) was reconstituted with a backdated date of 1 January, and the following units were included in it:
- Headquarters
- Armored Car Company
  - 1st Armored Platoon (*"Žaibas»*, *"Aras"*, *"Perkūnas"*)
  - 2nd Armored Platoon (*"Šarūnas»*, *"Savanoris"*, *"PRAGARAS"*)
- Armored Train Regiment
  - *"Gediminas"*
  - *"Kęstutis"*
  - *"Algirdas*
- Tank Battalion (newly established)

---

20 Some publications use the term armored platoon instead of armored squad.

21 The term Division in this case is not to be understood as a large military unit, but as the basic military unit of the self-armored department. By the consistency of vehicles and personnel it is assimilated to the force normally in charge of a Company with reduced strength.

- 1st Company - *"AUDRA", "Kovas", "Pagieža", "Pikoulis"*
- 2nd Company - *"Drąsutis", "Karžygys", "Smūgis", "GRIAUSTINIS"*
- 3rd Company - *"Giltine", "Kerštas", "Slibinas", "Galiūnas"*

The headquarters of the *Šarvuočių rinktinė* armoured and armoured units were in Kaunas, at the artillery barracks in the district of Žaliakalnis, also known as the Green Mountain, for the Armoured Car Company, and the Aukštoji Freda barracks for the Tank Battalion. In both barracks, garages, warehouses, workshops, and wooden buildings were installed to house the soldiers on duty.

On the evening of 17 December 1926, a coup d'état organized by the army took place, which took possession of the main centers of political and military power and arrested numerous officials. On that occasion, both armored cars and FT-17 tanks were deployed to defend the most strategic institutional and military locations.

Between 1926 and 1927, the Žaliakalnis barracks were renovated and optimized for the use and training of armored units. In the barracks, surrounded by a high masonry fence, there were 3 masonry buildings and the garages could hold 12 vehicles.

On September 16, 1927 the *Šarvuočių rinktinė* underwent a new reorganization following the downsizing of its departments, assuming the following personnel:
- Headquarters
- Armored Car Company
    - 1st Armored Platoon (*"Žaibas», "Aras", "Perkūnas"*)
    - 2nd Armored Platoon (*"Šarūnas», "Savanoris", "PRAGARAS"*)
- Armored Train Battalion
    - *"Gediminas"*
- Tank Company
    - 1st Platoon - *"AUDRA", "Kovas", "Pagieža", "Pikoulis"*
    - 2nd Platoon - *"Drąsutis", "Karžygys", "Smūgis", "GRIAUSTINIS"*
    - 3rd Platoon - *"Giltine", "Kerštas", "Slibinas", "Galiūnas"*

In 1933 6 Landsverk L-181 armored cars were ordered from Sweden, armed with a 20 mm Oerlikon gun and 2 Maxim 7.92 mm machine guns. They were delivered in 1934 and constituted the Armored Car Company structured on 3 platoons, each equipped with 2 L-181, which were deployed to the three cavalry regiments in Kaunas, Taurage and Radviliškis.

With the arrival of the L-181s, the old armored cars were used for training and later, in the mid-1930s, stored and held in reserve, although, due to obsolescence, their war value was virtually nil.

Unlike the FT-17 tanks and the old armored cars, the L-181s did not receive any name, but only a registration number, from KAM 6 to KAM 11.

Recognizing the age of the tanks in service, the Army leadership began the search for a suitable vehicle to replace the old ones. On 9 December 1933, the head of the Military Supply and Equipment Division of the Lithuanian Army and the contact person of Vickers-Armstrongs Ltd. signed a contract for the supply of 16 Vickers M1933 light tanks by 1934. This was a light tank equipped with a Vickers .303 (7.7 mm) caliber machine gun in a rotating turret, weighing 3.8 tons with an on-road speed of 56 km/h and off-road speed of 45 km/h and a crew of 2 men. It was essentially a tankette suitable for exploration.

Four tanks were to be equipped with two-way radios, these were the company commander's tank and the platoon commanders' tanks.

Deliveries of the 16 tanks began in September and were completed on 3 December 1934.

On 7 June 1935 in the barracks of Aukštoji Freda the 2nd Tank Company with 16 Vickers M1933 tanks was officially established. Even the Vickers tanks did not have a name but only a registration number. The organization chart of the Company was as follows:

- 2nd Tank Company - KAM 50 tank commander equipped with radios
  - 1st Platoon - Commander KAM 51 equipped with radio, KAM 52, KAM 53, KAM 54, KAM 55
  - 2nd Platoon - KAM 61 Commander with radio, KAM 62, KAM 63, KAM 64, KAM 65
  - 3rd Platoon - Commander KAM 71 with radio, KAM 72, KAM 73, KAM 74, KAM 75

In August 1935 the 1st Tank Company, equipped with 12 FT-17 tanks, was transferred from Kaunas to the newly built barracks in Radviliškis. In addition to three tank platoons, the company was supported by a fire department. Due to the mediocre operating conditions of the vehicles and their age, they carried out only training activities, even in support of infantry units.

On May 2, 1936 a new order was signed for the purchase of 16[22] Vickers M1936 tanks, an improved model of the previous M1933. The main changes concerned the suspension system, spring and no longer leaf springs, a more powerful engine of 80 hp and the thickness of the armor of the turret. As for the first order, four of the tanks were to be equipped with a two-way radio. The armament remained that of the first model, a Vickers machine gun cal .303.

During 1936, at the workshop of the *Šarvuočių rinktinė*, some important repairs were carried out on the engines of the FT-17, as a result of these interventions the speed of the tanks increased to about 13 km/h. In view of the state of the tank, the *"Giltine"* tank was not affected by the work and from that date was only used as a training tool.

In application of the reorganization planned by the leadership of the Lithuanian Army, in September 1937 the *Šarvuočių rinktinė* moved from Kaunas to Radviliškis, joining the 1st Company already stationed there since 1935. The personnel of the department at that date was about 500 soldiers, including officers, non-commissioned officers, graduates, soldiers and civilians.

Vickers-Armstrongs Ltd delivered the 16 tanks M1936 by the summer of 1937 and on 1 November the 3rd Tank Company was officially constituted, with the following organization chart:

- 3rd Tank Company - Commander KAM 100 radio-equipped tank
  - 1st Platoon - Commander KAM 101 equipped with radio, KAM 102, KAM 103, KAM 104, KAM 105
  - 2nd Platoon - KAM 111 Commander with radio, KAM 112, KAM 113, KAM 114, KAM 115
  - 3rd Platoon - Commander KAM 121 equipped with radio, KAM 122, KAM 123, KAM 124, KAM 125

Although deliveries of Vickers M1936 tanks had not yet begun, the Lithuanian Army leadership continued the search for new vehicles to further strengthen the armored forces. During 1936, major European armored vehicle manufacturers were contacted: Renault, Landsverk, Vickers-Armstrongs Ltd, Alvis-Strausser and Českomoravská-Kolben-Daněk ČKD. The Admission Commission Supply Division visited the Czechoslovak ČKD and viewed the new tanks that the company was producing or introducing into production.

The AH-IV tank and the TNH were presented to the members of the Commission. These vehicles were not considered suitable for Lithuanian needs, as they were too heavy and not very fast, besides being very expensive. The ČKD did not lose heart and its chief designer engineer Surin, who went to Kaunas to receive the requests of the Lithuanian tank drivers, succeeded in designing a tank that met the established specifications. On 26 May 1937 the order for the construction of a prototype of the new tank was signed.

On 26 January 1939 an LTL (Lehký Tank Litevský) tank, armed with a 20 mm Oerlikon-Solothurn gun and 2 Maxim M08 machine guns, and an LTH tank, this was the tank built by ČKD for Switzerland, were delivered for field testing. The tests were carried out in Kaunas, Prienai and Radviliškis, lasted until 21 February. On 10 March the LTH tank with some modifications was chosen and the

---

22 At least one source indicates that 18 Vickers M1936 tanks were ordered, but from the documentation consulted, 16 tanks were actually delivered.

purchase order for 21 tanks now called LLT (Lehký litevský tank[23]) was signed.

The contract called for delivery of the 21 LLT tanks in three lots of 7 tanks each, the first on 15 July, the second on 5 August, and the third and final on 19 August 1940.

With the arrival of the new LLT tanks the *Šarvuočių rinktinė* planned to establish in 1940 the 4th Tank Company and reorganize the existing ones as follows:

- 1st Company - 10 Renault FT-17
- 2nd Company - 15 Vickers
- 3rd Company - 10 LLT and 6 Vickers
- 4th Company - 10 LLT and 6 Vickers
- Training Company - 2 Renault FT-17, 4 Vickers, 1 LLT

The occupation of Czechoslovakia by the Germans in March 1939 led to total control of military production by the Germans. Although they did not initially stop tank exports, in 1940 the contract with Lithuania was suspended by the German military authorities and finally cancelled in 1941 by the Soviet Union.

The non-delivery of 21 LLT tanks prevented the Lithuanian military leadership from completing the reorganization of the *Šarvuočių rinktinė* as planned.

As of 18 September 1939 the *Šarvuočių rinktinė*, under the command of Colonel Babickas, consisted of the following units:

- Headquarters
- 1st Tank Company - Radviliškis
  - 1st Platoon - 6 FT-17 light tanks
  - 2nd Platoon - 6 FT-17 light tanks
- 2nd Tank Company - Radviliškis - 1 light tank Vickers M1933
  - 1st Platoon - 5 light tanks Vickers M1933
  - 2nd Platoon - 5 light tanks Vickers M1933
  - 3rd Platoon - 5 light tanks Vickers M1933
- 3rd Tank Company - Alytus/Taurage - 1 Vickers M1936 light tank
  - 1st Platoon - 5 Vickers M1936 light tanks
  - 2nd Platoon - 5 light tanks Vickers M1936
  - 3rd Platoon - 5 light tanks Vickers M1936
- Armored Car Company
  - 1st Platoon - 2 L-181 Landsverk at Radviliškis
  - 2nd Platoon - 2 L-181 Landsverk at Kaunas
  - 3rd Platoon - 2 L-181 Landsverk at Taurage
- Training Platoon

In implementation of the Ribbentrop-Molotov pact, on 17 September 1939 the Soviet Union invaded Poland and on 19 Red Army troops captured Vilnius. Lithuanian troops also participated in the attack on Poland, from 19 to 23 September, occupying the territory close to the border. On October 10 in Moscow was signed the treaty of mutual assistance Soviet-Lithuanian, among the clauses of the treaty was provided for the acquisition by Lithuania of the city of Vilnius and a fifth of the surrounding area, in exchange for granting the Soviet Union to establish five military bases in Lithuanian territory with the presence of about 20,000 Soviet soldiers. The Lithuanian government, after some resistance, had to accept what was imposed by the Soviet Union and sign the treaty.

On 29 October 1939 the Lithuanian troops entered Vilnius, welcomed by the cheering crowd.

Some units of the *Šarvuočių rinktinė* also participated in the advance, the 1st Platoon of the 2nd Company with Vickers M1933 KAM 51, 52, 53, 54 and 55 tanks, and the 2nd Platoon of the 3rd Com-

---

23 The final version of the LLT was to be armed with a 37mm Škoda cannon.

pany with Vickers 1936 KAM 111, 112, 113, 114 and 115 tanks.

After the reconquest of the territories considered as belonging to Lithuania since the war with Poland in 1920, and the return of the capital of the Republic to Vilnius, the armored units were redeployed to the following locations: Headquarters, 1st and 2nd Tank Companies in Radviliškis, 3rd Company in Vilnius.

The 3rd Company was quartered at the barracks at the foot of the hill dominated by Gedeminos Castle, previously occupied by the 3rd Polish Engineer Battalion. On 7 November 1939, while maintenance work was being carried out inside the garage where the Vickers M1936 tanks were parked, due to the fall of a kerosene lamp, a violent fire broke out that involved the tanks. 7 or 8 tanks were completely destroyed and 2 or 3 others were partially damaged. In practice at least 10 new Vickers M1936s were put out of action.

As a result of these losses, the 3rd Company was placed in a square position and an attempt was made to recover at least the damaged tanks.

According to the war plans drawn up by the *Lietuvos kariuomenės Sausumos pajėgos*, by the spring of 1940 only 20 Vickers M1933/1936 light tanks and 6 Landsverk L-181 armored cars were available and combatworthy, while the 12 Renault FT-17 light tanks and 6 armored cars from the War of Independence were destined for scrapping.

On 15 June 1940 the Soviet Union invaded Lithuania, the armed forces did not react as per government orders. The tanks and armored cars were stored by the Soviets and then distributed to the 615th Artillery Regiment and the scout battalions of the 179th and 184th Rifle Divisions belonging to the 29th Territorial Rifle Corps. Obsolete tanks and armored cars were dismantled, some light tanks were transported to a depot in Moscow, and others were used until the beginning of the war against the Germans in 1941.

The *Šarvuočių rinktinė* was officially abolished on October 27, 1940.

▲ The Renault FT-17 *"PIKUOLIS"* tank and its crew at the headquarters of the Ministry of Defense and the Army Chief of Staff on Gedimino Street in Kaunas on December 17, 1926.

CAMOUFLAGE, INSIGNIA, REGISTRATION NUMBER

The Renault FT-17 tanks delivered from France were used and in poor condition, some were painted uniform green and others were camouflaged. When they were repaired and reconditioned they were repainted in a uniform brownish green matte color. The Vickers M1933 and M1936 light tanks were painted in uniform olive green.

The Landsverk L-181 armored cars were camouflaged with rust red and yellow ochre stains on an olive green base. The armored cars that participated in the War of Independence were more complex. When the Izhorsky-Fiat was captured it was painted in uniform olive green, then it was camouflaged with ochre and reddish brown patches, surrounded by a thin black border, on a medium green background. The Ehrhardt *"Savanoris"* sonderwagen seems to have been camouflaged already at the time of its capture, from the photographs it can be seen that at the beginning of 1920 there was a mottled camouflage, probably ochre and reddish brown surrounded by a thin black border, on a dark green background.

The other 4 armored cars Ehrhardt-Behelfspanzerwagen seem to have been originally painted in a uniform color, probably a light gray-green, but later, in the early '20s, they were repainted with a camouflage similar to that of the *"Savanoris"* even if lighter.

No armored car or tank was ever painted with tactical symbols, not during the War of Independence and not even after the war until the Soviet invasion of 1940.

On armored cars that participated in the War of Independence, in addition to the name painted in white on the sides at the top center, a red coat of arms was painted, bordered in yellow, containing the Vytis (White Knight) a silver knight with gold spurs riding a silver horse, with a blue saddle and bridle decorated in gold, armed with a sword that he raises with his right arm above his head, while his left arm holds a blue shield adorned with a double cross. The coat of arms of the Vytis was painted on the sloping armor on the sides of the driver's station on all Ehrhardt-Behelfspanzerwagen, while on the *"Žaibas"* the coat of arms was in a reduced format and painted on the sides of the casemate under the name written in white.

On the Renault FT-17 tanks, in addition to the name, the Vytis coat of arms was painted on the plates on either side of the driver's access hatch.

On the Landsverk L-181 armoured cars the Vytis coat of arms was not painted, but the symbol of the columns of Gediminas was painted in white, placed on the sides of the armoured car, just after the access hatches, and on the rear inclined plate.

Also on the Vickers M1933 and M1936 tanks the Vytis coat of arms was not painted but the Gediminas columns were painted, always in white color and positioned on the sides of the turret. Initially it was painted on 4 sides but later, towards the end of 1939, the symbol painted on the front of the turret was removed.

All Lithuanian armored vehicles were registered by the Ministry of Defense - *Krašto Apsaugos Ministerija*, with the acronym KAM followed by the number painted on the front of the vehicle. The armored cars of the War of Independence received the numbers from KAM 1 to KAM 5, although it seems strange that, as there were six vehicles in service, all six were not registered. No such number was ever painted on the armored cars, however.

The Landsverk L-181 armored cars received the numbers from KAM 6 to KAM 11, the number, example KAM 7, was painted in white at the bottom of the front of the vehicle while at the rear was only painted the number of the armored car, example 7 always in white, much larger in the center of the inclined plate at the bottom. The Renault FT-17 tanks were identified by a name written in white on the sides of the casemate and by a serial number ranging from KAM 1 to KAM 12. From the photographs, however, it does not appear that these numbers were ever painted on the tanks. Specifically these were the registration numbers assigned to the FT-17: *"AUDRA"* KAM 12, *"Kovas"* KAM 1, *Pagieža* KAM 11, *Pikoulis* KAM 7, *Drąsutis* KAM 4, *Karžygys* KAM 2, *Giltine* KAM 8, *Kerštas* KAM 3, *"Slibinas"* KAM 9, *Galiūnas* KAM 5, *Smūgis* KAM 10, *"GRIAUSTINIS"* KAM 6.

The Vickers M1933 and M1936 tanks were identified by a KAM plate number followed by the number, written in white on a black rectangle painted on the sloping plate of the vehicle's front end, while at the rear only the much larger white number was shown on a plate installed on the left. The M1933 tanks were probably initially registered with a number ranging from KAM 1 to KAM 16, as can be seen in numerous photographs, while for the M1936 there is a photograph where there is a KAM 91 tank and therefore these tanks should have had a different numbering from the final one.

Between 1938 and 1939, however, all vehicles of the 2nd and 3rd Companies were retargeted with the new numbers assigned to the various platoons, as described in the text on the history of the *Šarvuočių rinktinė*.

▲ Tankers' badge from 1931

► Leather helmet used by tankers and motorcyclists of the Lithuanian Army from 1923 to 1940

►► The *Vytis*, The White Knight, is the coat of arms of Lithuania where, on a red background, there is a silver knight with golden spurs riding a silver horse with a blue saddle and bridle decorated in gold, armed with a sword which he raises with his right arm above his head and holds a blue shield decorated with a double golden cross.

▲ The armored car Erhardt Behelfspanzerwagen M1919 no. 4004 delivered to the Lithuanian Army by the Allied Control Commission on 29 January 1920 and renamed "*Aras*" (Eagle).

▲ The armored car Erhardt Behelfspanzerwagen M1919 n. 4026 delivered to the Lithuanian Army by the Allied Control Commission on January 29, 1920 and renamed "*PRAGARAS*" (Inferno) together with another identical armored car with the two crews lined up in front in the early '20s. In the photograph you can see very well the "Vytis", the coat of arms of Lithuania, painted in color on the sides of the armored car.

▼ The armored car "*Sarunas*" with its crew in the barracks.

▲ The armored cars Erhardt Behelfspanzerwagen M1919 *"Perkunas"* and *"PRAGARAS"* in barracks with their crews.

▲ The armored car *"Zaibas"*, at the head of a column of vehicles and military personnel that includes the *"Sarunas"* and another unidentified Erhardt Behelfspanzerwagen M1919, travels up Parodos street in Kaunas on April 16, 1920 (from "Lietuvos kariuomenė laikinojoje sostinėje 1919-1940 m.", op. cit. In bibliography).

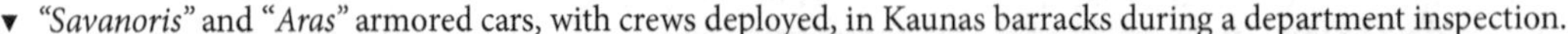

▼ *"Savanoris"* and *"Aras"* armored cars, with crews deployed, in Kaunas barracks during a department inspection.

▲ One of the rare photographs where you can see the back of the Erhardt Behelfspanzerwagen M1919 armored car taken in 1921

▼ Left, the armored car *"Perkunas"* with its crew during an exercise in the 1920s (https://laikas.tv3.lt/lt/info/8647/lietu-vos-sarvuociu-rinktine-arba-sarunai-drasuciai-galiunai-ir-pagiezos). On the right, the armored car *"Savanoris"* in barracks. In the photograph note well the "Vytis", the coat of arms of Lithuania, painted in color on the sides of the armored car, a winged knight with his sword extended upward

▲ All five Erhardt Behelfspanzerwagen M1919 armored cars in column on a Klaipėda road in 1924. From the photograph it can be seen that the first armored car, the *"Savanoris"* captured by the Lithuanians from the troops of Gen. Bermont, is different in the shape of the hood and the turret, cylindrical instead of rectangular as in the other four armored cars.

▼ *"Aras"* and *"Savanoris"* armored cars with Renault FT-17 *"Kovas"* and *"AUDRA"* light tanks, and their crews, on duty at the headquarters of the Ministry of Defense and the Army Chief of Staff on Gedimino Street in Kaunas on December 17, 1926.

▼ The armored cars *"Savanoris"*, *"Aras"* and *"Zaibas"* in maintenance at the garage in Kaunas in 1922 .

▲ Renault FT-17 "*Slibinas*" (Dragon) tank during winter exercises, in cooperation with infantry, in 1934.

▲ Souvenir photo of officers, noncommissioned officers and tankers around the Renault FT-17 "*Kovas*" (Tower) tank in the barracks

▼ The Renault FT-17 "*Slibinas*" tank surrounded by tank drivers during training.

▲ Souvenir photo of officers, noncommissioned officers and tankers around the Renault FT-17 "*AUDRA*" (Storm) tank in the barracks (www.plienosparnai.lt/e107_plugins/forum/forum_viewtopic.php?3820.70)

▼ Souvenir photo of officers, noncommissioned officers and tankers around the Renault FT-17 "*KERSTAS*" (Vendetta) tank in the barracks (www.plienosparnai.lt/e107_plugins/forum/forum_viewtopic.php?3820.70)

▼ A platoon of Renault FT-17 tanks, you can recognize in the foreground the tank "*GRIAUSTINIS*" (Thunder), engaged in overcoming relief near Kaunas in 1924 (from "Tankai Lietuvos kariuomenėje 1924-1940 m.", op. cit. in bibliography)

▲ Two Renault FT-17 tanks engaged in mid-1930s summer maneuvers along with infantry (www.facebook.com/senosfoto-grafijos/photos/lietuvos-kariuomenės-lengvieji-tankai-vicker-nemune-prie-kauno/10150468278841976)

▲ Three Renault FT-17 tanks during summer maneuvers in the mid-1930s.

▼ Renault FT-17 "*Kovas*" and "*AUDRA*" tanks, with their crews, at the headquarters of the Ministry of Defense and the Army Chief of Staff on Gedimino Street in Kaunas in winter 1926.

▲ A group of Renault FT-17 tanks, you can recognize the "GILTINE" (Death) tanks of the 3rd platoon and the "*GRIAUSTI-NIS*" tank of the 2nd, during inspections by crews during maneuvers in the Gaižiūnai area in the early 1930s.

▼ Renault FT-17 *"Slibinas"*, *"KERSTAS"* and *"AUDRA"* tanks, belonging to 1st Platoon, in Kaunas in 1926 (from "Tanks in the Lithuanian Army 1924-1940", op. cit. in bibliography).

▲ Two Renault FT-17 tanks during an exercise (www.plienosparnai.lt/e107_plugins/forum/forum_viewtopic.php?3820.70)

▲ Two platoons of Renault FT-17 tanks deployed at the end of summer maneuvers at Radviliškis in 1935 (www.plieno-sparnai.lt/e107_plugins/forum/forum_viewtopic.php?3820.70)

▼ Deployment of Renault FT-17 light tanks, tankers and soldiers of other arms, during the parade on September 8, 1937 in Radviliškis (from "Tankai Lietuvos kariuomenėje 1924-1940 m.," op. cit. in bibliography)

▼ Renault FT-17 tanks parade in front of military authorities at the end of a ceremony, Kaunas early 1930s (from "Tankai Lietuvos kariuomenėje 1924-1940 m.," op. cit. in bibliography)

▲ Vickers M1933 tanks and Landsverk L-181 armored car during the 8 September 1937 parade at Radviliškis (from "Tanks in the Lithuanian Army 1924-1940", op. cit. in bibliography)

▼ Landsverk L-181 KAM 7 unarmed armored car engaged in exercise (http://tankfront.ru/neutral/litva/photo.html)

▼ Training of crews in the maintenance of Landsverck L-181 armored car (http://tankfront.ru/neutral/litva/photo.html)

▲ The population enthusiastically welcomes Lithuanian soldiers and tank drivers from the Vickers M1933 KAM 51 tank on October 27, 1939

▼ Landsverk L-181 KAM 5 and KAM 6 armored cars, belonging to the 1st Hussar Regiment, with their crews, at the funeral ceremony of General Sylvester Žukauskas on November 28, 1937 in Kaunas.

▲ Left, Landsverk L-181 KAM 9 armored car engaged in an exercise, note the machine gun in anti-aircraft position (http://tankfront.ru/neutral/litva/photo.html). Right, an ex-Lithuanian Vickers M1933 tank abandoned by the Soviets in 1941 following the German advance on Kaunas (http://tankfront.ru/neutral/litva/photo.html)

▼ Vickers M1933 KAM 51 tank, equipped with radio, of the commander of the 1st platoon of the 2nd company (www.facebook.com/senosfotografijos/photos/lietuvos-kariuomenès-lengvieji-tankai-vicker-nemune-prie-kauno/444131441975)

▲ The Vickers M1933 KAM 7 tank in service in the 2nd company (from "Tankai Lietuvos kariuomenėje 1924-1940 m.", op. cit. in bibliography)

▲ The 1st platoon of the 3rd company, equipped with Vickers M1936 tanks, can be recognized the KAM 102 tank and the KAM 101 radio tank, parade in Radviliškis in 1939.
▼ Vickers M1933 KAM 53 tank in service with 1st platoon of 2nd Company.

▲ Vickers M1933 tanks drive along the street in front of Vilnius Cathedral during the parade on 16 February 1940, leading the KAM 54 tank followed by the KAM 52 (from "Tankai Lietuvos kariuomenėje 1924-1940 m.", op. cit. in bibliography)

▼ Platoon of Vickers M1933 tanks waiting to begin the advance towards Vilnius between 19 and 23 September (from "Tankai Lietuvos kariuomenėje 1924-1940 m.", op. cit. in bibliography)

▲ Left, Vickers M1933 KAM 51 tank, 1st Platoon, at the head of the column of tanks and truck troops waiting to advance across the Polish border between September 19 and 23, 1939 (http://icvi.at.ua/forum/698-760-1). Right, Vickers M1933 tank column waiting to advance across the Polish border in the Vilna region between 19 and 23 September 1939 (http://tankfront.ru/neutral/litva/photo.html)

◄ Vickers M1933 KAM 51 and KAM 55 tanks, from 1st Platoon of 2nd Company, engaged in overcoming a stretch of swampy terrain.

◄ The Czechoslovakian Praga LTL (lehky tank litevsky - Lithuanian light tank) ordered by the Lithuanian armed forces in 21 units in 1939 but never delivered due to the occupation of Lithuania by the Soviet Union.

▼ Vickers M1936 tanks of the 1st Platoon of the 3rd Company, KAM 104 and KAM 105 can be recognized, drive along Pilies Street in Vilnius Old Town on October 29, 1939 after entering the city.

▲ Vicker M1933 KAM 15 and KAM 16 tanks filmed crossing the Nemunas River near Kaunas.

▼ Vickers M1933 KAM 14 tank during a phase of initial training.

BIBLIOGRAPHY

Books and other publications

- AA.VV., "*Tankai Lietuvos kariuomenėje 1924 – 1940 m*", Centro di cartografia militare delle forze armate lituane, 2015.
- Vytauto Didžiojo karo muziejus, "*Vytauto Didziojo Karo 2018 metais Almanachas*", Centro di cartografia militare delle forze armate lituane, 2019.
- Vytauto Didžiojo karo muziejus, "*Lietuvos kariuomenė laikinojoje sostinėje 1919–1940 m.*", Centro di cartografia militare delle forze armate lituane, 2020.
- Viljandi Muuseum, "*Eesti Iseseisvuse Sund*", 2008.
- Bernardo E., "*Armored Cars in The Baltic States 1918-40*", 1991.
- Kirvelaitis T., "*Lietuvos Respublikos kariuomenės šarvuočių rinktinė*" (Tesi di Laurea), 2013.
- Estonian War Museum, "*Estonian War of Independence 1918-1920 - Estonia's Allies*", 2019.
- "*Lithuanian Military Digest*", n°5, maggio 202.

Websites

- www.waralbum.ru
- http://it.topwar.ru
- http://tankfront.ru
- www.foto-history.livejournal.com
- https://strangernn.livejournal.com
- https://kv-bear.livejournal.com
- http://nelsonlambert.blogspot.com/2012/06/estonian-armour-1919.html
- http://aviarmor.net/tww2/armored_cars
- http://estonia-paradise-of-the-north.blogspot.com
- https://panzerphotos.com/vickers-6-ton
- https://issuu.com
- http://eag.vanatehnika.ee/ewarmee.html
- www.militaar.net
- https://www.ra.ee/fotis
- https://ajapaik.ee/photo/106443/soomusrugemendi-mehed-koos-soomusautodega/
- http://www.kool.ee
- www.live.warthunder.com
- http://latviansmilhistory.blogspot.com/2009_10_24_archive.html
- https://www.la.lv/foto-militaras-parades
- https://www.zudusilatvija.lv
- https://www."*Sargs*".lv/lv/latvijas-neatkaribas-kars
- https://spoki.lv/vesture/Latvijas-Autotanku-brigade
- https://tanks-encyclopedia.com/latvian
- https://www.antik-war.lv
- https://vesture.eu/Latvijas_armijas_Tanku_divizions
- https://www.plienosparnai.lt/e107_plugins/forum
- https://www.savaite.lt/lietuva/1263-nepriklausomybsgynjainuoaiboikiboxer.html
- https://forum.axishistory.com
- http://www.landships.info/landships/car
- http://arecibo-camo.blogspot.com/2011/03/"*PRAGARAS*"-"*Perkunas*"-ir-kt.html
- https://laikas.tv3.lt/lt/info/8647/lietuvos-sarvuociu-rinktine-arba-sarunai-drasuciai-galiunai-ir-pagiezos
- https://picturehistory.livejournal.com
- https://it.knowledgr.com/07331036/EsercitoLituano(1922)
- http://latvjustrelnieki.lv/lv/fotografii-95943/period-borjby-za-nezavisimostj-latvijskoj
- www.securityguard.lv/2020/01/blog-post_30.html
- http://arecibo-camo.blogspot.com/2010/04/lt-ginkluote-sarvuoti-traukiniai.html